I Used to Think Vegans Were Dicks

I Used to Think Vegans Were Dicks

E. L. Armstrong

PRESS

PRESS

Published by Vulpine Press in the United Kingdom in 2022

ISBN: 978-1-83919-470-2

www.vulpine-press.com

Dedication – Mother Mary

No actual, published book would be complete without an apology to my mother for using such a vulgar title. Sorry Mum, but I'm seeking to get people's attention so…yeah, sorry because I know you save cussing for the really bad stuff – but climate change is really shitting bad so, sorry.

Love you.

Contents

Preface
Vegan Spoils Christmas

Christmas 2018, A Vegan Walks into My House...

My brother-in-law's girlfriend is German. Chill out Cleese – that's not where I'm going with this. We were due to be nine for Christmas Day of 2018; myself, husband, two children, mother, mother and father-in-law, brother-in-law and said girlfriend. So as I said, she's German and lives in Sydney, Australia. Sydney is home to a lot of progressive, wellness knobheads and trend-following, Insta-posing millennials (it's basically Australia's California) who decided to buck against the Antipodean carnephilia and go plant-based. Dicks.

So, this vegan was coming for Christmas at my house with her on-trend nonsense. Such a dick. I had to make joyless, vegan gravy. Did she turn up bearing vegan lebkuchen? Well, yes, but don't believe for one moment that sweet gestures make dents in my intolerance. Despite being a decent cook, I had very few vegan dishes in my repertoire and certainly not within my traditional Christmas fare –

birds, pigs, butter on vegetables – you know the drill. It all resulted in me whining to anyone who'd listen and my poor mother (the one who is flustered by vulgarity, let alone veganism) tearing all round the supermarkets seeking a vegan nut roast so we could all sit and eat different things at my, so graciously hosted table. Eye. Roll.

27 December 2018, My Birthday

I get a birthday card from my lovely friend emblazoned with,

'How do you know someone is vegan?

Don't worry, they'll tell you'

Evidently, I was such a whiny bitch about my brother-in-law's girlfriend bringing her faddy eating to my dinner table, my friend thought our little in-joke would amuse me. Ha ha ha – vegans really are dicks.

December 2020, Sometimes It Takes a Death Plague

My husband and I are down to eating meat only once a week. I suggest trying to perfect a similar recipe without meat in it…and then we were meat-free.

It's true. I one hundred per cent thought people who were vegans were right dicks. Since then, something miraculous happened and I was forced to examine whether perhaps it wasn't the vegans who had the copyright on this particular quality…

I would like to be totally transparent from the outset: I am not a climate scientist – although maybe that's a good thing given that none of us are actually listening to climate scientists. I am, however, a person who loves science and life and nature; I am a self-declared naturalist that has to check they mean naturalist rather than the people who *really* like being naked. Dicks. I should *cough cough* probably mention that I sat the extension paper for GCSE Biology about 20 years ago and that I used to live in the woods (without a tent, not an exaggeration) but please contain yourself if my statistics are slightly off and my statements are not peer-reviewed. My mission is to spread awareness and levity – reputable scientists are all available for detailed explanations.

What is a Vegan?

A vegan (*vee·gn*) is a person who opposes the consumption of *all* animal products. If it comes from an animal, you can't eat it, drink it, wear it or even lick it. For true vegans, you can't even have honey because it's made by bees – who are part of the animal kingdom. So, in essence, vegans think Winnie the Pooh is a domineering bee overlord who gives zero shits about the 100 Acre Wood's inhabitants. Dick.

What is a Dick?

Look, I'm trusting that you know what a dick *literally* is but in my world, it occupies a special socio-linguistic space. Granted, it's not very sophisticated to be using the male phallus to illustrate something that is *not good* in 2022, but do you know what, let's agree to split the difference given that women have had the mucky end of the stick since we invented agriculture – ok?

Hold up Emma. You lured us in with your cussing and piqued our interest on climate issues – don't spoil things by going ANYWHERE near gender inequality.

Back to my definition. A dick is someone in society who *just can't be fucking nice.* My mother has been wont to suggest that people who are dicks had mothers who, 'didn't slap their legs enough when they were little' but given that it's not the 1980s, we no longer condone corporal punishment and we mustn't take this analogy literally.

A dick is someone who, say, might pull out of the Paris Agreement because they *know best,* someone who might approve a new Cumbrian coal mine in the middle of a climate crisis because they were distracted by really expensive wallpaper samples; a dick. Equally, a dick can quite readily be a person who is rude to restaurant and supermarket workers, someone who is vile to their subordinates at the office and who buys your kids really noisy toys at Christmas because they think it's 'funny.' Oh, and online trolls. They're vile. A simple rule of thumb is: if it's not nice, it's a dick thing to do.

Why Specifically Did I Think Vegans Were Dicks?

Because I'm such a nice, tolerant, open-minded person, I felt it important to have a loud opinion on the dietary choices, made from a position of trying to do right by the planet and its inhabitants, of other people. God – what dicks!

When I unpick why I felt so ragey about someone else's pile of lentils, it makes for uncomfortable viewing. I was cross at the vegans because:

They are a somewhat marginalised and maligned group in society and it's easy to take pot shots at a convenient scapegoat (especially if they're weak from a protein deficiency).

One, solitary vegan made my Christmas catering a bit more complicated.

Vegans were deliberately (dicks) making me feel (at least subconsciously) uncomfortable about my own dietary choices and their impacts.

After the aforementioned, uncomfortable reflection (fuck, maybe *my* mother didn't slap *my* legs enough) I have to concede that there is a possibility that it was me being the dick all along. Ouch.

Desmond Ford was a Eurocentric, white guy who said something along the lines of a wise man (obviously a man, always a man) changes his mind, but a fool never does. In an attempt to stop being a judgy vegan-basher (vasher?) I'd like to introduce you to what made me stop, look, listen and experiment (disastrously) with vegan cheese.

Who Even Am I?

Scientifically speaking, I'm a nobody, and my own children would struggle to pick me out of a line-up unless I was waving carbohydrate-based snacks at them. I am just a person, like every other person who has ever existed, who lives on our shared home. This makes me spectacularly well-placed to write a book about an issue that's already affecting *everybody*. Wondering why I have such a lady boner for the planet and ecological stuff? When I was in my early twenties, I was all geared up to enter academia when I had a quarter life crisis and realised that if I spent my working life indoors it just might kill me. As a result, I took the suitably mature, not to mention financially imprudent, steps to become an outdoors education instructor and ran away to live in the woods. I was completely skint but did a job I loved with people who were awesome and I lived outdoors in beautiful British woodland. It was heaven. Admittedly I wore a lot of green at a time when that *All Saints* look was already passé and my personal grooming went to shit but, my God, it's pretty special to see the seasons change and wake up to fresh air and birdsong.

Hang on there, Captain Planet.

Yes?

You said you lived in the woods. How the hell does that work? Where do you shit?

Why is this always the first question that springs to mind? Conveniently, when you live in the woods, much like the fabled bear, you defecate in the woods. Personally, this meant I used an outdoor toilet called a long drop. I'm playing a touch fast and loose with the word toilet here, I confess. A long drop is a long, narrow hole in the ground that you shit in. Might as well be up front about that.

Oh Christ, my mind's eye is watering from that visual.

Well, you did ask. I also brushed my teeth, showered, partook in the occasional sweat lodge, ate all of my meals, drank lots of coffee and got rained on a fair bit. It was bliss.

How does being a bitch about your sister-in-law and defecating al fresco relate to the climate emergency?

Glad you asked. Well, it doesn't especially, but the really important things you need to know about are to follow. I hope to tell you (or remind you if you're good at pretending you don't know) about how bad things are because of the way we're treating our planet, which in case you're a total bellend, is both wrong and fucking stupid, because we all live here. All of us. Everyone. Ever. Subsequently, even if you're a nasty piece of work who never replaces the empty loo roll, or, indeed, hoards it so others have to wipe their backsides with kitchen roll/moss, you should at least have a self-motivated interest in how we might survive what has been labelled the next *Great Dying* – and the dinosaurs will confirm that the last one was less than enjoyable – although Dennis Quaid would probably be thrilled to reprise his role in *The Day After Tomorrow*/any film that would have him.

All rude words and joking aside, it's my hope that after reading this you will know and you will care that we are really fucking up (sorry, Mum) with an even more naïve hope that maybe, just maybe, enough people will be moved to stop kicking seven shades of shit (the origins story of *Fifty Shades of Grey*?) out of our environment. There is a tipping point at around about the 25% mark with social movements – if just a quarter of the population can get on board, we might be able to save the cheerleader/the planet/ourselves.

Maybe.

Chapter 1
Oh God, Everything's Fucking Terrible!

Wendell Berry wrote, 'expect the end of the world. Laugh.' Humour and doom don't seem like the likeliest of bedfellows but I'm hoping it'll sugar this particular pill. Or at least enable you to show off to your friends that you finished reading an entire book on science. Either, or.

What is about to follow is not good. Not good in the manner of having been so drunk that you wake up with sick in your ear, a mouth that tastes like you've licked a Megabus seat and the devastating feeling that you're going to need to make multiple apologies. Not good in the best ever *British Understatement of the Year Award* way.

Full. On. Shit.

I am going to be candid here even though you'll think me a dreadful pessimist: we are *really* fucking shit up and it may already be too late to change this/fix things. As Oliver Milman cheerfully notes, 'almost all the evidence suggests that we have left it too late to avoid suffering on a huge scale.' Great.

What sort of stuff are we talking about? Well, everything, as it happens. Glaciers, ice shelves, rainforests, water courses, sea levels, fish stocks, carbon budgets, defaunation, humanitarian crises, biodiversity…truly, I could fill the whole book with gloom of the highest order and still only have scratched the surface (of the planet we broke because we suck). However, I have a sneaky suspicion that you're mostly here because you like a bit of swearing, or were seduced by the possibility of some vegan-bashing, so I'll get back to those sanctimonious dicks. Kidding. (Remember I've reconsidered my position – their dick status is currently under review.) To follow are a few of the big things we *all* (yes, even Donnie) need to read, digest and respond to accordingly. There is no longer any question of 'believing' in climate change. It has changed and is continuing to do so. Positioning climate change as 'something I don't subscribe to' puts you squarely in the Flat Earthers' camp. You do not want to be in that camp – it's full of eejits. And cockwombles who are, if anything, worse. Moreover, because we didn't pay enough attention to the 'change' bit, we're now splashing about in a full-blown climate emergency. Fun times.

The truth is inconvenient, our house is on sodding fire and unless we take dramatic, substantial, collective action, every last one of us risks dying – from climate disaster –

obviously we're all going to die anyway, but hopefully more like Rose in *Titanic* rather than the poor bastards in *The Impossible* (i.e. the wet way). For clarity, Rose, as an old lady, having lived a long and happy life rather than Rose on a floating door in the freezing sea and with a dead boyfriend hanging off the side of said door. That would be shit.

Bor-ing!

Well, actually not that boring. The science is rather dramatic – and scientists don't really *do* dramatic because they prefer covalent bonding and peer-reviewed papers. Lads.

Trigger warning: the following information will probably give you eco-anxiety which the American Psychological Association describes as 'a chronic fear of environmental doom.' But I'm firmly of the belief that we need to be shocked and appalled at how blithely we are trudging towards an ecological disaster of a scale that is unimaginable to our faithful 'business as usual' mindset.

To follow is a small selection box of some of the causes and impacts of the environmental issues we're all complicit in. Yes, even if you drive a Prius. If you drive a Tesla, you really shouldn't feel so smug; everyone thinks you're a knob.

Planetary Warming

Every time we use a car, fly in an aeroplane, turn on an electrical item powered by coal-generated electricity or buy a rude book about vegans, we emit (either directly or indirectly) carbon (amongst other things) into the Earth's atmosphere. The more carbon we have in our atmosphere, the warmer global average temperatures become, because carbon dioxide traps the heat from the sun's rays and boom, you can grow bananas in Bexhill. Trees suck some of this yucky carbon dioxide in through their leaves and helpfully swap it for oxygen for us to breathe during photosynthesis, but yeah, we keep cutting trees down to enable us to have lots of Big Macs so…awkward. That's right, the beautiful green giants are trying to help us and we literally just burn them. Explain that logic to a 5-year-old if you want to feel really crummy about yourself.

Additionally, carbon dioxide is just one of the so-called greenhouse gases that are causing the planet to warm up. Not 'so-called' because I'm sceptical but because this is what smart people say when first introducing a term – I'm so 'here for' greenhouse gases. That came across poorly. I hate them. They're breaking my home. I'll shut up now. Other culprits include methane and nitrous oxide (that one the kids all do in those little silver canisters down the park on a Saturday night) which are both a great deal more potent but, thankfully are a smaller proportion of the gross stuff we pump into the air we breathe. Despite being British, and therefore secretly a bit thrilled by the prospect of warmer winters and being able to staycation without freezing my tits off in July, this is horribly bad for the planet. The Paris

Agreement has agreed (never would have guessed) to try to keep global temperature increases to well below 2 degrees and preferably to 1.5 degrees in an attempt to limit some of the god-awful consequences of damaging the environment so egregiously. Then *someone* *ahem* went and pulled out of the Paris Agreement because, apparently, they knew best and didn't want some poxy climate pact to limit the ability of their country to tear through the agreed carbon budget at a rate of knots. Whilst that *someone* isn't *anyone* that people should look up to for policy ideas or try to emulate, unfortunately that didn't send a very helpful message to a world trying to get to grips with the need to come the fuck on with the saving the planet already. I really hate it when *some people* are dicks. In case you think I'm being alarmist, the Climate Change Committee, which is an independent body and not affiliated with the vegan conspiracy, has advised the UK government to prepare for a 2 to 4 degree global temperature increase. These tiny temperature increments are anything but tiny when measured by the damage they will do. Please note that I am also not affiliated with the vegan conspiracy.

See, I knew *there was a vegan conspiracy!*

Relax – the vegan conspiracy is a conspiracy. As in, it's not real. Vitamin B12 deficiencies make you ineligible for conspiracies. More on this later.

Pollutants

There are many different ways in which pollution is injurious to planetary, wildlife and human health. Industry is outrageous in the amount of polluting it does – cement manufacturers, for example, are real dicks on this score. Luckily, industrial pollution doesn't count nor incur penalty because you know, money talks to politicians so that industry can keep making money while your urban neighbours can't breathe thanks to air pollution levels that make cigarette smoking look like sucking on vitamin sticks. The WHO estimates that around 7 million people die annually from small particulate pollution which really doesn't agree with the human respiratory system – but, you know, money. Before anyone gets all high and mighty with me about how industry provides jobs for working people and taxes for national projects, I'll remind you that industry *uses* people as a resource to be *exploited* and (much like a former Chancellor's wife) keeps most of its profits off-shore, in clever tax-avoidance manoeuvres, so you can hush your noise.

Agricultural Emissions

Transportation is really bad for our planet – running as it does almost exclusively on fossil fuels, but there is actually a far more culpable sector, which is also dependent on transportation, so it is arguably doubly damned. 15% of greenhouse gas emissions originate from animal husbandry. As George Monbiot informs us, 'farming, whether intensive or extensive, is the world's major cause of ecological destruction.' In particular, cows fart a lot because they are ruminant beasts – basically they eat a lot of grass (calm down, not *that* grass) and in the process of digesting such an unpalatable foodstuff, their guts produce a lot of methane (one of our greenhouse pals). This means not only are their farts smelly, they're also causing the planet to heat up at a rate that is 80 times faster (over 20 years) than carbon dioxide. Methane is really bad news and a really big problem that isn't really given as much (hot) air time as it should be. Cynics might suggest that is because, if you're taking issue with methane emissions, you indirectly (but importantly) have beef with farmers – potentially beef with beef farmers. This is confusing and risky because it is essentially trolling the hand that feeds you. More on that cosy conundrum later. At this juncture I should point out, using the Bigot's Defence, that one of my good friends is a farmer and the only thing he's guilty of is being unable to shake off a friend like me. But to be clear, I don't hate farmers, nor am I going to use this book to bash them. That's why we invited the vegans.

Ocean Acidification

Whilst this may sound like an ill-advised *Red Hot Chilli Peppers* comeback, this is simply where we interfere (interfere in the manner that certain national treasures like to interfere with children and vulnerable adults) with the pH levels of the oceans and given that the oceans cover about 70% of the Earth's surface and contain about 97% of the Earth's water, this is kind of a big deal. Acidic seas are bad news and markedly less enjoyable to paddle in at the beach – have you seen the state of the grandma's legs in *Dante's Peak*? It also leads to the bleaching of coral reefs and whilst this is bad news for Australian tourism, more importantly, it fucks the coral ecosystem, leading to its death. Coral reefs are oceanic hotbeds of biodiversity, in addition to serving as a kind of undersea breakwater, protecting coastal areas from ocean storm surges. The chances of recovery are slim too and Jonathan Safroen Foer agrees with a lot of scientists when he says that 'we cannot save the coral reefs.' This, dear reader, is why we can't have nice things. Mind you, it may be that the Great Barrier Reef stands a slightly better chance under Albanese than it ever did under dear old ScoMo.

Biodiversity Loss

What even is biodiversity? It sounds like some sort of equal opportunities bollocks for nature.

This makes me really, really sad. (The biodiversity loss, not your cynicism.) Lots of really cute animals with big old eyes and baleful expressions are already approaching extinction. Polar bears (ice thaw), orangutans (so we can glug loads of palm oil), pangolins (so we can make snake oil medicines) and snow leopards (because we're nothing if not industrious). These are the lead singers of the animal world and they get great reviews and plenty of posters on teenage bedroom walls. Far less cute but no less important is the dwindling biodiversity of plenty of 'invisible' species that are slipping away unnoticed. By slipping away, I mean being exterminated by, you guessed it, humans. Less biodiversity is a sign of an ailing ecosystem. At present, if we were to calculate the biomass (the weight of our collective arses) of all mammals on Earth, 96% of it would be humans and farmed animals. In case the maths is beyond you, that means only 4% of all of the mammalian backsides on Earth are wild ones. This problem is even more egregious for insects. Agriculture and its phenomenally heavy use of pesticides is the main driver of this loss – Germany recently recorded a 75% loss of insect species in some areas.

Germany really needs to get its shit together.

Nope – you're still not thinking fourth dimensionally. National borders mean precisely dick in the climate crisis. Just because Germany has bothered to go round and count its insects because it's such a wonderful country (sucking up to my vegan sister-in-law) and has more data, does not mean we can breathe a heaving sigh of relief.

Mind you, pretty nice to breathe deeply without risking wing-ed nature in your airways.

Nope. Bugs are absolutely critical to our ecosystems and there is no 'work around' once we've wiped them out. We can't use technology to science the shit out of having no natural pollinators. We are not (I repeat *not*) going to encourage people to invent robot bees to try and replicate the work of our striped beasties. Oh Christ, now I'm giving people terrible ideas. Please, for the love of God, do not start inventing robo-bees.

Variety really is the spice of/key to life on Earth. More on the insect apocalypse later.

Sounds fun. Can't wait.

Food Waste

Food production is a frighteningly large contributor to climate change. Moreover, it's estimated that globally, about a third of all food grown or reared gets wasted. This admittedly includes everything from wonky carrots being rejected by retailers to the pathetic (plastic, obviously) bag of rocket at the bottom of my dew bin swimming in its own juice and us all regularly having eyes bigger than our bellies, but still – a third! All food production is carbon and water heavy in its resource use, its transportation and its disposal.

According to WRAP, global food waste produces more greenhouse gas emissions than all commercial flights. Helpfully, rotting food decomposing in landfills also emits methane which is a shame – largely because it's hurting the planet and because so many thousands of people don't have enough food, it seems a little bit rank to just throw stuff out. Food waste is, as Tim Lang says, 'a cultural act of planetary stupidity.' I'm going to voice an unpopular opinion (it's unlikely to be my last) – I think companies such as Deliveroo, Just Eat, Uber Eats and so on are culpable in this – they make it possible for people to easily reject the 'home food' languishing in the fridge in favour of all of the delicious takeaway food – without even having to speak to another human. Food waste upsets me in large part because I'm tight but also because my wonderful grandma, Mona Kathleen, grew all her own vegetables and I've seen how much sodding work goes into it. It's a crying fucking shame. Worst of all, it's easily avoidable.

Topsoil Erosion

This sounds like an especially niche corner of the adult entertainment market but is actually just another (yes, another) effect of a few thousand years of tilling the land. Repeatedly ploughing furrows (the grooves where the seeds sit) in fields kicks up dust and, over time, bits of it blow away and there is less and less soil available to plough that's any good for growing the crops on which we depend on for survival. No dirt means no dinner. Previously useful arable land is losing its mojo – and this will be further exacerbated by rising temperatures – dry soil is easier for the wind to spirit away and places with delightful names such as The Fertile Crescent (Iraq, Syria, Lebanon, Palestine, Israel, Jordan, and Egypt) and America's Breadbasket (US Midwest) will have no option but to rebrand as Barrensville and You're Going to Fucken' Starve. This will be inconvenient for starters (*well, there aren't going to be fucking starters, Emma, if everyone's starving*) and is likely to drive humanitarian issues such as resource refugees through the chuffing roof.

Ice Thaw

Our creeping global temperature increase is leading to a lot of cold places thawing and unhelpfully sending their meltwater everywhere. Water will find its own level and eventually end up in the sea/flooding all the nice beaches. Ice is melting at the polar ice caps, the permafrost is thawing (which is even releasing anthrax – for once we can't come at the Russians for chemical weapons turning up in *Zizzi's*) and there's also a lot of methane stored in the ice – methane is the cranky big sister of carbon dioxide and she is proper livid. Finally, there's a charming thing called the albedo effect. This is the ability ice has to reflect heat because of its light colour. Ice considerately reflects some of the sun's heat back out into space meaning we don't get as scorchio-d as we might. However, if more of the ice melts/gets all sooty from our dirty pollution and the wildfires we've caused by being dicks, the reflective potential of ice is lost thus speeding up global temperature increases and ice melt.

Which brings us neatly to…

Rising Sea Levels

Have you ever noticed how lots of big cities are sited on accessible bits of coast or large rivers and estuaries?

What, the Bangladeshi Delta? Yeah, give a shit.

Well, yes. But also parochial little hubs like New York City and London.

Ah, fuck.

Yes. Loads of places that are full of wealthy Westerners are going to get completely *disappeared* under the sea – but with no cheery crustacean to sing to us while we all drown. London presently relies upon the Thames Barrier to protect most of the Greater London Flood Plain (AKA London – I'm not making this up – that's what it's called) from tidal and storm surges. It is a magnificent piece of engineering but NASA's figure of an increase in sea level of 3.3mm per year is really going to burst the London property bubble and the Thames Barrier won't be much help. We aren't talking about a few hundred thousand brown people in Asia who we don't care about getting flooded here (well, we are, but obviously that isn't very motivating) – what we are talking about are a good number of the major metropolises and huge chunks of coastal living space being completely underwater.

Welcome to Miami

Miami is sinking. No, not in terms of its monied corruption and moral bankruptcy, but in terms of something moving from being on top of the water, to under it. With typical American can-doism, authorities have announced that they can manage rising water (the sea level). Now I'm all for a positive attitude but unless they are King Triton, I'm pretty confident the sea doesn't take well to being 'managed.' Florida, in its entirety, is vulnerable to and already suffering from the effects of climate change. Rising sea levels, denuded Everglades, repeated battering by storms and a scarcity of freshwater sources are going to plague Florida over the coming decades. Plenty of wealthy Floridian counties are spending astronomical amounts of money to save this playground of the rich – often literally passing the problem on downstream/to where the poor people live. Miami is not going to be saved which is upsetting for its wealthy residents but ruinous for those who are poor. The reality of it is that the US is likely to experience mass climate migrancy in the next 20 years.

Extreme Weather Events

After Hurricane Katrina hit New Orleans in 2005, it took a fucking unacceptably long time for the US federal government to send meaningful assistance to its own citizens – the beleaguered residents of New Orleans. Approximately 30,000 people were left stranded in the superdome sports arena. The hurricane took more than 1,800 lives and cost somewhere in the region of $106 billion. Famously, Kanye West called President Bush out on not caring about black people (the cynic in me can't help but wonder if response times might have been quicker were it The Hamptons that were decimated) and sure, he didn't exactly issue an emphatic denial but, if an enormous humanitarian disaster is allowed to unfold on US soil, what the fuck chance do other places stand of enduring, weathering if you will, increasingly common extreme weather events? Storms are getting bigger and stronger, storm seasons are lasting for longer and the unpredictable nature of weather systems makes them nigh on impossible to plan for, let alone mitigate.

Feedback Loops

That thing at a gig when the guitarist gets too close to the amp when s/he's mic'd up and you hear that awful whining noise that hurts your ears?

Climate feedback loops are a whole new level of visceral pain. So, what is a feedback loop? When we, say, raise the temperature of wooded areas through our carbon emissions, we make them more prone to wildfires. Those wildfires burn for longer and over larger areas which in turn create soot and ash. That ash then lands on arctic ice making it look less than Insta-ready – the dark colour of the soot causes more of the sun's heat to be absorbed by the ice (rather than being reflected as it would have been) and thus causing the ice to melt faster. This then causes sea levels to rise. The warmer temperatures cause increased humidity which increases the regularity of storm events and tidal surges but because the sea levels are already higher because we caused those wildfires to start with…it's pretty much the worst game of Snakes and Ladders ever: all snakes and no ladders.

A future peppered with extreme weather events means that we will be bouncing/swimming from one shitshow to the next – unable to tidy up from one disaster before being pummelled by the next. It's what scientists call a clusterfuck. Ok, so the scientists don't say that, but they are grievously concerned about feedback loops and God knows what other horrors we risk unleashing by continuing to do a job on the natural world.

I have a question.

Shoot.

Must you swear so much? It's vulgar.

I hear you and even my Australian husband finds my potty mouth a bit much sometimes. But, climate change is an *emergency*. You don't have a go at paramedics for using their sirens when they're en route to save someone.

Woah there, with your Messiah Complex.

This is serious so I'm allowed to employ a bit of cursing for emphasis. Plus, I like swearing. If you prefer I could lecture you on navigation and magnetic declination? At present declination in Greenwich is positive with an inclination of…Let's press on.

So, to recap, here are some of the really large turds floating on the surface of the pool we're all paddling in:

Rising global temperatures caused by too much carbon dioxide, methane, nitrous oxide etc. in our atmosphere = some people will freeze to death, some will be roasted – both will be intense.

Rising sea levels = people will drown *en masse* and just you ask Rose if you think that's a fun way to go.

Increasing prevalence of extreme weather events = not that funny time it hailed in June or you saw a daffodil in January but massive *The Day After Tomorrow* storms which will ruin everything up to and including your weekend BBQ plans. They will also (neatly) impact most heavily the already economically marginalised – people who have been historically shat on are in line for more horror. But rich, white people won't be immune either – March 2021 floods in Sydney, anyone?

Logically, because humans are just so awesome, our increasingly polarised society is all too ripe for the civil discord/humanitarian shitshow that will inevitably increase as resources become more scant. Think mass migration as people are forced to flee areas that can no longer support human life.

Ocean acidification (can't have fish), soil erosion (can't have chips).

Wait, what? Back a step – no fish and chips? But we always have fish on a Friday!

The more damage we continue to do, the more we trigger unforeseen and unstoppably damaging feedback loops. Feedback loops are bad. Very. Fucking. Bad.

Just who decided it was a good idea to haphazardly stack piles of shit adjacent to all the fans?

I could pontificate at length but in brief, oil companies, farming corporations, the aviation sector and every single one of us.

Why Do I Feel Qualified to Lecture/Terrify/Upset You?

I have spent more time in nature than you've had hot dinners and the core of my work has been sharing skills and knowledge of a disappearing world – a disappearance being compounded by climate change. This makes me feel bad for my part in it and sad for what it means for the world. My own vashing (I'm totally trying to make vashing happen) *volte face* was prompted by a realisation of HOW BAD SHIT IS. Many people are now aware of the obscene amount of plastic dumped in the ocean thanks to David Attenborough and Hugh Fearnley-Whittingposh and I'd been trying out ways to cut our household plastic consumption for a couple of years. Not to brag (I am bragging) but we had switched to glass bottles of milk, reusable nappies, ditched cling film and plastic bin liners for recycling (I know, who'd be that dense?). Unoriginal as it is, I think the real gut-roller was having children and answering their adorable (inane, never-ending) stream of questions: "Mummy, why is your bottom so hairy? (Loudly, publicly) Are you doing a big poo or just a wee wee?" When little people earnestly ask you about single use plastics and why you drive a dirty, diesel, carbon-spewing van, the most willfully obtuse among us are herded towards uncomfortable self-interrogation.

Bad Mother

I am practising a somewhat anachronistic style of parenting. My children spend much of their time outdoors, they have never held an iPad or smartphone and they are home educated. This isn't a hashtag humblebrag.

It sure as hell sounds *like a humblebrag, Emma.*

No seriously, it's not, it's called exposition – I'm setting the scene. And another thing. When I say, "I enjoy toast at breakfast," everyone needs to get off their keyboard-mounted steed and quit wailing about the virtues of porridge. I'm just saying I like toast – I am not judging you for your choice to have porridge. Also, I'm hungry from feeding a baby all night – I have porridge *and* toast. Life is a rich tapestry and we need many different threads. Not Reddit ones though as they're full of keyboard warriors. Moreover, I don't even have a Twitter account but perhaps, if I did, my handle should be: The Girl Who Shat in the Woods. Has a certain ring to it.

Anyway, in part *because* I've worked as a conventional classroom teacher in a secondary school, I choose not to send my children to school and recognise that being able to make this choice is a huge privilege. (Although teachers who home educate are potentially the canary in the coal mine here. Just saying.) The other part is that I so sincerely value an education based in the natural world that the SATs race seems particularly anathemic for me; I can't bear it. In a vain and old fashioned, Pasternakian belief, I want my children to know what the living things which surround them are called and why they matter, and more to the point, why fronted adverbials do not. I'd rather my children could identify six tree species than be able to tell me the order in which Henry VIII shagged his way through Court. What greater privilege can I give my children than instilling in them the same sense of peace and wonder that I find in just being outdoors?

I knew I could smell the weird on you.

I *shat* in the woods but my kids not attending conventional school is what set your alarm off?

Also, it sounds a bit like you're bashing teachers here...

A. I'm not that stupid and B. I'm married to one so, it would be a touch awkward. What I can't abide by is the refusal to distinguish between the people working in a system (wonderful) and the constraints of the system itself (deeply flawed). I'll also be discussing farmers later on so do try to leave some harumphing gas in the tank before you get to that part. Additionally, a reminder that the charming people who make the delightfully undeliverable educational policies in Whitehall almost exclusively attended very different sorts of schools. They send their own darling offspring to very different sorts of schools. They are also, overwhelmingly, the sort of people who will be best placed to ride out climate change with less of an impact on their quality of life.

Jesus, that chip on your shoulder must weigh a lot.

It's ok, I've got strong legs (the place you are advised to bear weight when carrying heavy loads, such as expedition backpacks). I'm good at carrying stuff.

Hang on. Armstrong? That name sounds familiar...

Neil Armstrong, first man on the moon. Big deal, nice guy, no relation.

I was thinking of the bike guy actually. The one who got cancelled. Hard.

Ah, yes. He didn't do many favours for the Armstrong name in terms of veracity and believability in the non-fiction book sector. Luckily, my surname is through marriage because I just didn't have the energy to challenge that corner of the patriarchy that day. Back to my failings…

Mea Culpa – Me a Dick, Uh

I am a climate criminal. I do lots of things to hurt the planet every single day. These hurts include but are not limited to: driving a big, dirty diesel van because I have too many kids, having too many kids, buying peppers in plastic because I can't be arsed to find a set of scales with the printer labels working at Tesco, rinsing bowls before they go in the dishwasher, having long showers, leaving sockets on, charging my phone overnight, shopping on Amazon, using plastic dog poo bags, wearing disposable contact lenses, putting clothes into landfill because they have massive holes in and I simply must avoid charity shop volunteers judging me, consuming dairy (I'll level with you – it's mostly cheese which is the worst one because it takes so much milk to make a teeny bit of cheese), wearing seal fur (I'm kidding, who the fuck wears fur in 2022?), using noxious cleaning products to mitigate infrequent housework and generally arrogantly assuming I have the right of dominion over planetary resources because…we all do.

Like so many good ideas (female subservience and repression, batshit notions of good and bad), much of our planetary arrogance stems from the good book. No, not *Fifty Shades*, the *Bible*. Genesis teaches us that we get to have dominion over all the Earth and make micro plastics when we wash our fleeces, have turtles think carrier bags are jellyfish and have Antipodean surfers call washed up tampon applicators 'beach whistles' which is bizarrely funny but also horrifying (largely because I have a mental image of Sam from *Home and Away* saying, "toot toot" into one). The absolute domination of planet Earth by a single species is not because we're turbo lads and not really entirely because of our opposable thumbs. In short, organised agriculture led us here, by enabling us to control sections of the planet to raise food on and have too many babies which we could then actually feed. We have (yes, yes, I know I'm complicit here) overpopulated the Earth. More to the point we have overpopulated it with the wrong sort of people – Americans and Europeans use far more resources and emit far more harmful shit than people in less economically developed societies. I am the wrong sort of people. My children are mostly likely going to be the wrong sort of people.

We have fucked our planet and, just to clarify, our planet is not an abstract, separate, other place. If Covid teaches us nothing else it should remind us that there is no escape –

there is no running away to somewhere apart, somewhere untouchable. Unless you're a celebrity or an advisor to the Prime Minister. There isn't a soul who can escape the realities of what a 2/3/4/5 degree temperature increase will mean for our home. Sure, the really rich folks will have it easiest but everyone and everything is going to suffer. A lot.

In short (*er, there was nothing short about that*), the ecological disaster in which our planet finds itself is an utter shitshow. A really, really bad one. Of the scale and magnitude that makes me want to crawl into my microfibre-shedding, ocean-trashing bed and snarf chocolate made from cocoa washed by the tears of a near-extinct orangutan until I don't feel the hurt any more.

Oh God, you're so dramatic.

Yup. I blame *Captain Planet* (he's a hero) for sowing the seed that has finally brought me to my senses.

I hope I can convince you to be at least mildly vexed in due course.

What You Can Actually Chuffing Do:

1. Spend less time mindlessly scrolling through people you aren't mates with in real life. 28 minutes on Instagram is equivalent to 166 metres of driving and when was the last time you *only* spent 28 minutes making yourself feel cruddy about your own, unphotogenic existence?

2. Drive your car fewer miles – your waistline and asthmatics will thank you.

3. Don't buy drinks in plastic bottles. Take one with you or be a bit thirsty – you'll live.

4. On that note, take a packed lunch when you're travelling/working. It'll save you money too.

5. Fly less. No one is entitled to spaff aviation fuel all over the stratosphere with impunity – no matter what the low cost airlines' marketing would have you believe.

6. Go for a walk – good for your mental and physical health and a reminder that the frenetic pace we live at isn't good for all concerned.

7. Grow something – doesn't need to be *River Cottage* in your bedsit. Plant some cress and remind yourself we aren't separate from the natural world.

8. Avoid plastic as best you can.

9. Compost if you have the space. The veggies/cress you grow will thank you.

10. If you are blessed with good health, show some fortitude/stubbornness/nouse and put one or two extra jumpers on and turn the heating down/off.

Chapter 2
Am I the Dick? Weapons of Mass Consumption

The Importance of Being Self Indulgent as Fuck

I'm pleased to see that you've removed your copy of *I Used to Think Vegans Were Dicks* from your charity shop pile and are back with us. I appreciate that Chapter 1 wasn't exactly palatable and you may still be reeling from the existential threat I had to be such a knob and mention – like, dude, not cool. Eco-anxiety is a very real thing – in the same vein that Big Dick Energy (BDE) is very much *not* a real thing. Yes, you are a weapon – double entendre intended. This realisation/admission can take some getting used to and yes, it's another stick with which to beat our fragile mental health.

Great. Cheers, Emma.

Patronising hand-holding aside – seriously – be kind to yourself. It's not (wholly) your fault that you have been behaving like such a bell-sniffer.

Given that you've just received some pretty bad news (regarding the destruction of the natural world and how it's your own silly fault), you are hereby entitled to a little bit of wallowing time. The process of environmental awakening (God, can I hear my own dick self?) is a really painful and depressing one. Take whatever time you need to mope about, listlessly stare at the walls and ignore that urgent email from your line manager because, WHAT'S THE FUCKING POINT IN ANYTHING ANYMORE?! WE BROKE THE WHOLE SHITTING WORLD!

Now I know that the whole pandemic thing has been more than a little rough on our collective mental health, but I think it's really important to recognise the guilt we should (unless you're a sociopathic monster) feel regarding our complicity in breaking all the nice stuff. We have all done a lot of bad things. Sure, the Boomers were bigger dicks but at this point, keeping a spreadsheet seems like a poor use of carbon heavy mains electricity. Some people (me) really like to board the Malthusian Tragic Train and head for Shame Town. I think a good wallow – to make sure the message has sunk in and to check we're really paying attention now – is no bad thing, but we do eventually need to climb out of our pit of despair, so don't make the sides too steep.

When I fall down a doom-laden rabbit hole, I like to indulge myself by reading everything I can get my hands on about it. The husband finds it thrilling when I read out another titbit of misery so as to enable him to join my woe-wallowing and catastrophizing. Best. Wife. Ever! One such pleasant evening he'd had enough so I screenshotted a paragraph from the book I was reading and sent it to my ecologically-minded mate, whereby he replied:

'Haha – Yes it all is a bit bleak! It's easy to get bogged down. Little positive steps here and there. [thumbs up emoji]'

Cheerful moi responded:

'I'm still in the 'Greta was so sad she didn't speak for 3 years' phase. I'll get there.'

What's gutting is that even the nice publishing house who printed this book, are doing terrible things to the environment. Inks and glues pollute, waste margins are high in publishing and, er, you don't get books without chopping down and macerating the shit out of some poor, carbon-sequestering trees. Moreover, *some* authors aren't as successful as they were predicted to be and the surplus/unsold copies of their books are just pulped (using energy) thus wasting all the energy used to make them. In effect, by convincing you to part with money you earned (probably in a way that hurts the planet) in order to educate you about how we're hurting the planet, I've inadvertently made you hurt the planet. More.

This book should come with free beer.

Probably.

We all, especially in the Western world, consume too damn much. Too much food, too much water, too much fabric, too many electricals. (I knew I'd lose your respect if

I didn't get my singular and plural qualifiers right.) We drive too many cars and take too many flights. We are all doing the considerate neighbour thing really badly – even those of us who try to be dicks/vegans.

Speaking of other books on the environment, this book seems a bit on the short side actually. Cat got your tongue, Emma?

Of Mice and Men is only 30,000 words…

Yeah, but that's a literary classic, a critically acclaimed novella – it's allowed to be short.

As someone who's taught *Of Mice and Men* to countless, reluctant teenage boys, trust me, it ain't *that* short.

Hang on, you've been a normal *teacher too? I thought you hated schools?*

Weren't you paying attention? I've already mentioned that. But, yes, I have also been a (non school hating) secondary English teacher (we all have to eat) amongst other things including, a barmaid, an editor and a cleaner in a prison and almost certainly the Master of None. Full time writing seemed like the next logical step. Oh, and I don't hate schools, I just worry about narrow curricula and that they aren't able to let kids be outside nearly enough. But as I was saying, most books on the environment and climate change are long, dry, dense and lots of other things that put off both habitual and non readers alike. In addition, how many times have you actually read an IPCC report? Exactly. The scientists who are face-palming at our *Don't Look Up* strategy, are doing the hard, sciency stuff but the message delivery system needs some work. David Wallace-Wells writes that, 'there is no single way to best tell the story of climate change, no single rhetorical approach likely to work on a given audience, and none too dangerous to try. Any story that sticks is a good one.' I am proposing that we need to try *funny* – because apparently credible scientific writing isn't lighting enough fires under enough arses. Also, just because you might be learning something, doesn't mean you can't have a little bit of fun while you do. Unless you're being taught *Of Mice and Men* by me, apparently.

IPCC, What?

The IPCC is the UN's Intergovernmental Panel for Climate Change. They have worked to bring together and collate all the good science we know to be true about the climate and have repeatedly explained that if we could just hold still for a minute they'd like to get the thorn out of our paw before we get tetanus. They have, in effect, written several (really damning) school reports about how badly you behaved in Geography, Science *and* History class and now you're trying really hard not to let your parents read it. Luckily, these reports are phenomenally dense what with all the planet death science and ain't nobody, policy makers, governments and lay people included, who's got time to read that. If you think I'm exaggerating/infantilising you, I'll just let you know that Page 9 alone of the *Summary for Policymakers* has

12 footnotes, the jazziest of which runs, 'RCP-based scenarios are referred to as RCPy, where 'y' refers to the level of radiative forcing (in watts per square meter, or W m-2) resulting from the scenario in the year 2100.'

Sorry Emma, please continue to treat me like a child.

As I was saying, many books on climate science then utilise much of this data (partly because it's good data and partly because why would you conduct your own research when this narrative gold is so readily available?) to inform their discourses on climate science and how everything is irrevocably broken. That's fine and lovely but there aren't many of us who have the time or the inclination to make head or tail of people that don't speak human – this is, I fear, where the message is being lost. I wouldn't presume to patronise you, but I will assume that you glazed over in Anthropocenic Apocalypse Science 101 and so hope to translate some of the information that is critical to our survival but is ostensibly as boring as balls.

The Sixth Sense (Assessment Report)

In April 2022 plenty of hardworking scientists were mightily cheesed off that all the graft they'd done for the *IPCC Sixth Assessment Report* (IPCC AR6) went largely unnoticed by the mainstream media, in part because most people aren't massively into hearing that they and their planet have no future and in part because Putin is a dirty great war criminal. IPCC AR6 is not the first time the IPCC has tried to speak to our parents about how we are definitely going to tank our exams. It's worth noting that whilst the full report is purely science-based, the *Summary for Policymakers* is politically influenced because it requires a consensus between the members who are trying to make themselves look a little bit better/reduce their chance of getting grounded with no Wi-Fi for a month.

The IPCC AR6 is a really, really important document. It's the *Haynes Manual* for how we might save the planet and a massive lecture about consequences, young lady, if we don't listen to Mother (Earth). I have some form in reading interminable technical documents having worked for a technology house, where I edited interminable technical documents. It weighs in at a modest 3,675 pages but even I glaze over reading this tome – and I really like climate science and ecological misery-lit. This is a fundamental issue with the climate crisis – at one end it's all way too technical and at the other, people supergluing various body parts to various parts of the transport infrastructure. I don't think that a bit of levity somewhere in the middle is too much to ask for.

Tiptoe Through the Tarp Pegs

I mentioned earlier that I used to live in the woods. This is not a euphemism – for most of my twenties I actually *lived* in the woods for the purpose of teaching wilderness, indigenous technology and survival skills. I slept under a small tarpauline which meant I got a bit damp when it rained, but also enjoyed 24/7 fresh air. One of the skills I have taught countless (predominantly male) adults is how to kill, skin and butcher a rabbit. Ending an animal's life is not pleasant. There is always a degree of gritting your teeth and taking a deep breath before doing the deed – I get this same moment of wobble when dispatching a fish I've caught with a club or even ending the life of some injured wildlife I know is suffering.

JESUS CHRIST – the woman who wrote this book is a FUCKING MURDERER! I thought she was meant to like nature?

It is the moment when you are going to bring to an end a living thing's existence – while you carry right on existing. It's uncomfortable and it should be. Somewhere around the time of the Industrial Revolution, people left their connection to the life cycle on the land when they went to the towns and cities. (Sure, we could pursue a slightly more in-depth historical analysis here but climate change is a ticking, so I'm paraphrasing.) We have become increasingly detached from the realities of meat ever since. This detachment allows us to consume without conscience and meat has moved from high days and holidays to three times a day. The wealthy have always consumed plenty of meat but the decrease in the relative cost of food and the increase of incomes (despite persistent and endemic deprivation – not to mention a cost of living crisis) means that meat is much more accessible to many more people. Its production is vastly more 'efficient' in 2022 – almost exclusively at the expense of animal welfare. Vegetarians and vegans are not ok with this. Vegans adopt a stronger position (some say, extreme). Heavens, I know it seems a bit rude to say that people who eat meat and dairy are ok with animal mistreatment – but this is the reality. If one eats meat, one is complicit with animal suffering. You'd be forgiven for thinking that not consuming meat is adequate to get you off the hook – but I have bad, vegan-shaped news for you – it's not. If you consume any animal products, you are complicit with animal suffering, with animal cruelty.

I actually have a dog, two cats and a parakeet called Jemima who recites dirty limericks.

Bully for you, bellend. I should probably inform you that a New Zealand study asserted that owning a medium sized dog has a heavier carbon footprint than an SUV.

Loving *some* animals is arguably weirder than being full on, meat is sweet, no matter the feet. People get really upset when they see pictures of dogs in cages in meat markets in China. Let's be real – people in the West like a bit of 'harmless' old-fashioned bigotry and being able to joke that Chinese people eat anything. But have you ever seen a baby cow? My dog is cute, but she hasn't got an ounce on a sweet little calf that can also lick its own nostrils. The selective carnivorism the West prides itself on smacks of hypocrisy, exceptionalism and a feeling of wholly unqualified superiority. (I've suggested the West omits this from their Tinder bio.) Whether you eat a pet dog, grass-fed cow or pole-caught bluefin tuna, something had its natural life span cut short so you could have dinner. For farmed animals, they also likely endured a shit life – one you wouldn't want your pet dog to endure – and a really ugly death. Wild animals may be spared the stress and restrictions of agriculture but that's probably small consolation when someone shoves a hook through your face and a pickaxe in your eye to haul you into the boat. Just a thought. I'll wager you found those last couple of sentences a bit extreme, too much, unnecessary.

I'd counter that perhaps our dependence on and addiction to animal protein and products is a bit extreme, too much, unnecessary.

A Flexible Fable

'Nothing is so painful to the human mind as a great and sudden change' – Mary Shelley.

I am no chef, but I'm a decent home cook (*alright, Delia*) even by my husband's high culinary standards. Friday night is curry night and I make a delicious (completely inauthentic) cauliflower jalfrezi as it's his favourite and a nice way to end the week. Recently, I mixed things up a bit

— I cooked it in the slow cooker rather than my stained old cast iron pan on the hob. (The hob runs on fossil fuels which are heating up the planet and I also read that the fumes from the hob are poisoning my baby so, you know, winning.)

Hubs was not happy. I'd fucked about and tampered with his favourite. Now I really was a dick. Maybe even winning the coveted *Dick of the Week* award. (What, you don't have this in your household?) To clarify, my husband is an incredibly nice person who just wanted to eat his sodding curry without someone meddling with the thing he enjoys so much. What it demonstrates though is how acutely emotional our responses to food are. Food is so intrinsically tied up with feelings of home, childhood, familial love, care, celebration, nurture or the absence of the above that we all have a tendency to be dicks about it sometimes.

There is going to be a monumental change in our food landscape one way or another. If we continue to pursue our consumption of animal products in gross quantities, we will increasingly drive climate change that will smash the shit out of us, or we will change what and how we eat to mitigate some of the damage we've done and to attempt to heal our battered world. Resistance is both pretty futile and pretty unethical. Sometimes, there are more important things than being able to eat whatever the damn-well you please.

Wow, Emma, you're really starting to sound like a dick. I liked sweary, meat-eating Emma better.

I know but don't shoot the messenger – I'm only 36 – plenty of people before me could have tackled this crisis so we could have had unlimited wheels of cheese. Blame the Boomers – they broke the housing market too FYI.

But What About Pizza?

Yeah, pizza. I love pizza. (Really, who doesn't? If you know someone ambivalent on this matter, question whether you want that energy in your life.) Every Saturday night is Pizza Night in my house. I'm a full pizza-wanker – I make my own dough, sauce: the works. I set the kids up with a little pizza-making station so I can stand and behold how, even though I'm clearly messing them up in a multitude of ways, they'll at least have warm, fuzzy memories of making pizza with Mummy. I love a pizza, they love a pizza and I love a meal that no-one has ever refused because they are a fussy little dick.

There isn't an easy way to say this but pizza is a problem. (Yes, I'm really going there.) Cheese isn't exactly helpful on our little crusade to save the planet so we have air to breathe and water to drink. Cheese is the third worst foodstuff in terms of climate impact – worse than pork and chicken – because it takes a lot of milk to make a little bit of cheese. To get milk you have to chop down the Amazon to grow grain and soy to feed to cows whose chewing, crapping and farting our old pal methane (worse for the atmosphere than that dick carbon dioxide) all over the shop means cheese is dirty – even before we've forcefully impregnated heifers on a loop and then taken away their babies soon after they give birth so the babies don't 'steal' the milk. We then take lots and lots of that milk to process into a modest amount of cheese which itself is energy-intensive and has unhappy waste to yield ratios. Then we grate it and "frinkle frinkle" (my toddler's words) the golden loveliness over a delicious tomato sauce on a cheeky little pizza base.

"But Mummy, are we never going to be allowed to frinkle, frinkle the cheese on our pizzas ever again? I want to save our planet but now I fucking hate you!"

So, I've got to ruin my children's lives – vegans are such dicks.

Veganism alone isn't going to dig us out of this mess, but it's inevitably got to play a large role. We have got to stop farming livestock the way we are – including its accompanying razing of rainforests to grow soybeans to feed to baby cows who can lick their own nostrils.

Change is a spectacularly difficult idea for us to get to grips with. Change is mostly scary and anxiety-inducing and the change that is coming features an awful lot of unknowns. For example, we know that a warming climate will cause sea levels to rise but we don't know whether it's just Mauritius that's going to be wiped off the map or the whole of the Bangladeshi delta too. Stupid, selfish scientists – it would be a lot more comfortable for me if they'd just make up their damn minds. Dicks.

Lesson of Less

Less is not very sexy – one of the reasons it's so hard to sell. You may have seen recent large supermarket ads stepping up/jumping on the bandwagon to tell us to eat *more* plants. Not *less* meat you'll notice. Capitalism is somewhat reliant on more, not less, forever and ever, Amen. I have a very rudimentary understanding of economics but even to my ignorant eyes, it's clear this system is, to coin a relevant phrase, unsustainable. We need to be sustainability pushers and one of the biggest changes we're going to have to come to terms with is less. Less stuff. Less food. Less travel. Less getting our nails did. Less.

Urgh, fuck this, I'm off.

Please don't go yet – it really takes a sunnier turn around Chapter 4, maybe.

Most of us throw uneaten food away. Most of us don't need a holiday to the Algarve in the actual, real sense of the word 'need.' Most of us could get off our arses and do a bit more walking and a bit less driving.

Many millions of people around the world – and indeed, in the UK, do not have enough. Pretty fucking tasteless for me to be preaching about less, eh? Except, one of the reasons so many don't have enough, is that we, my guilty arse included, have too much. The astronomical disparity of wealth in the UK alone is enough to turn anyone with a heart, full, textbook socialist. (N.B. – Obviously not hardline Tories – they are heartless – it's science.) Some people trebled their order of cut flowers to pep themselves up during Lockdown 1.0 whereas some people in the same city had to deny themselves a meal so that they had enough food to stop their children from going hungry. Marcus Rashford had to fight really, really hard to make the government (pretend to) give a shit about just this one issue of deprivation and wealth inequality. It's appalling. Horrifyingly, food scarcity caused by climate change will only compound this already shameful issue. Throw in a (giant bunny ears) Special Military Operation in Ukraine and we will know and feel the pain of systemic food shortages over the next couple of years.

There is no getting away from the fact that climate change, as the pandemic has done, will throw existing social issues into even sharper relief, with the wealthy able to buy more flowers/pay more for basic supplies to surf through future crises as they have this time. A hard truth we need to accept is the massive change in age-old industries and vocations that will have to happen to avoid rendering huge swathes of the planet uninhabitable. This includes allowing the rich to behave with impunity.

Thanks a lot, now I feel like a dick. I feel this product has been mis-sold.

Spitting on the Children

I have too many children. Both in the practical sense that I can't get my shit together because I have too many children, and in the moral sense in that I saw a meme on Facebook that said the single worst thing you can do for the planet as a Westerner is to have an additional kid. Yeah, so ballsed that up. The flip side of my Weasley brood is that it's forced me to be a bit less selfish in the way I look at things. I feel a little bit more driven by my obligations post-kids rather than motivated by my stonking sense of Western entitlement. Only a little bit – woe betide you if you are the dickhead who parks in my parent and child space when I've been soothing a teething baby all night. Further personality flaws aside and clichéd as it is – having kids has changed me. Mostly because I've created little eco monsters. In my misguided attempt to make my offspring ecologically aware, I've turned them into tiny, repetitive (oh, so repetitive) eco-Gestapo. They pummel me with interrogations about why I grabbed the peppers in the plastic that I know isn't recyclable ("BECAUSE MUMMY'S A FUCKING *HORRIBLE PERSON*, POPPET, OBVIOUSLY!").

Speaking of Kids, Educating Them Can Save the World

It should obviously be a no-brainer that we educate *all* children rather than only the ones who have tails (I'm looking at you, the 'we're just making sure it's safe for them to return because we care so much about the prospects and safety of women' Taliban) but even in 2022 (and I'd wager the same will be true in 2032) we aren't getting this right. Girls being equally educated (I still can't believe we're having to talk about this one) directly impacts our mission to save the planet. The better girls' educations are, the later they enter marriage and the fewer children they have – ergo – fewer people creating emissions *and* girls get treated like humans rather than chattel for dudes to marry. Really, I struggle to see a downside to this (and yet, the Taliban, sigh). Good old climate change disproportionately affects girls as they are more likely to be pulled out of education to help mitigate the effects of climate change on a family – especially in impoverished households and communities. So, it's really important that we educate girls to the same level as boys and as this is confusing for some (male) people, let's have a simple blanket rule that we support and fund universal education until, say, 16, globally.

Slow down there, Malala. That's going to cost a lot of money.

It really is. Fortunately, I've thought of an abundant funding stream. I mentioned previously my namesake who was the first man on the moon. The first of 12 humans to ever set foot on the moon – all of whom were men. NASA's gender equality record aside, is it really a good use of funds, to be spending trillions of dollars on performative science in space? If it were any other agency, the cost to benefits ratio would be indefensible. So why all the heavy spending? It's mostly about prestige and not about scientific advancement – that's just what the public are told to justify why they can't have universal education or clean energy solutions because all the money was spent on sending yet another man into orbit. And don't get me started on space tourism.

Space Cowboys

Ok, I've already started on space tourism. We really need to stop, yesterday, space tourism. Space tourism is something that implausibly wealthy people cooked up to make implausibly large amounts of money, court prestige and throw tonnes of greenhouse gases into the ailing atmosphere. This has got to be up there with seal clubbing and child brides in terms of ethics. Firstly, it burns thousands of gallons of fuel because, even very expensively engineered rockets are reluctant to leave Earth's atmosphere, and so you need a hell of a lot of fossil fuel to persuade them to do so. Secondly, I have a very real worry for rich people.

By permitting them to be so spectacularly over-indulged, it risks them becoming complete and utter arseholes who nobody ever stands up to or says no to – it's a slippery slope from your team enabling you to treat yourself to a space flight to allegedly helping you traffic underage girls to your mansion. I think rich people may just need saving from themselves. Let's start saying no to them. Thirdly, all that money we're throwing at space programmes and letting rich idiots/megalomaniacs go on space joyrides could be far better used for universal education.

Didn't you use a NASA statistic in Chapter 1, Emma?

Ok, they can keep their Earth Sciences Division, but the space nonsense at least has to go on hold until we clean up this mess first. Perhaps you feel it's unfair that the US should have to fund global education, just because it currently spends loads on a space programme – in 2021 the US spent $54.59 billion in order to further science, (mumble mumble) better understand something, (mumble mumble) that will be of zero benefit to most people. Also, the US has a lower literacy rate than Cuba – maybe more investment in public education would be a better bet.

But, the Economy!

To follow is a short list of people who will be screwed by the necessary societal changes required to mitigate some of the effects of the climate crisis (please note, I couldn't get everyone on this list and get to bed on time, so if you feel like you're also about to get fucked over by our shared future, please email me at emma@IUTTVWD.co.uk and be sweary):

Livestock farmers

Oil industry workers (obviously, could give a shit about the stupidly wealthy oil-magnates)

Car industry workers

Coal miners

Many manufacturing jobs – impacting low-paid workers globally.

When the British farmers are all going under because you convinced people to eat less meat and they can't afford to pay their mortgages, will you feel like a right clever dick?

So – awkward truth: if we all decide to be awesome and move to a more sustainable, plant-based diet, a lot of really hard working farmers who are also nice people who are just trying to feed their families and live their lives will cease being able to draw an income from rearing livestock. Ouch. This is awful. That isn't faux empathy by the way. This is a very real, coal face reality for humans who deserve to have their voices heard. However cruel and callous it may seem though, a bunch of livestock farmers going under is small fry…that's how bad this is. That really nice lady with lots of children who farms sheep in the Yorkshire Hills – yeah, awkward but she needs to *not* do that. (The farming part –

we have already agreed that it's too late with the lots of children thing.)

I'm conscious I sound a bit unfeeling at this point but let me elaborate.

Lots of people losing their livelihoods is terrible. Rotten. Miserable for them and theirs. It may even cost lives – the suicide rate for farmers is already shocking. There will be people who are utterly desperate. However, should we continue in our arrogance and inflexibility, far more people will lose their livelihoods and lives because of climate change. Hill sheep won't survive a 3 degree temperature increase in fleeces which will turn them into roast lamb before they hit the shop shelves. I promise I'm not going after ruminant farmers because I've watched *Cowspiracy* and methane is over 80 times more powerful at warming the atmosphere than carbon dioxide. I'm mentioning them because even wholesome (and really lovely) people like those I'm alluding to, cannot continue to rear livestock at our current rates. And that's before we even get into the industrial meat production slurry pit of shame.

Yeah, but we already do Meatfree Mondays…

Which is so lovely for your conscience but precious little else and we don't have time for me to be cute. Everyone in the country doing Meatfree Mondays at tea time is a piss-ant drop in the over-fished ocean.

Thanks – Now I feel like a dick.

The Lamb Is Sure to Go

According to an April 2022 headline, Northern Ireland will have to lose (eat/cull and not replace) 1 million sheep and cattle in order to meet its climate targets. A million. For argument's sake let's say 500,000 lickle baa lambs and 500,000 moo cows. The farming sector has to reduce its (especially damaging) methane emissions by 50%. This is all rather admirable and exciting if you're a climate activist. It is decidedly less so if you are a Northern Irish livestock farmer. I am (clearly) a huge proponent for legislating climate targets (mostly because asking people politely hasn't quite got the results you'd hope) but we also need to make proper (not Westminster, lip-service) provision for people who are livestock farmers. Simple maths (of which even I am capable) tells us that farmers aren't farming so many heads of sheep and cattle because they want more animals to look after, but rather it is an economy of scale necessary to extract a living from a capricious and economically unviable industry. Subsidies presently prop up livestock farming and one could argue there are better ways to spaff public money.

This feels a bit like a watershed moment. For so long we have lived under the (false) assumption that animal protein was the only solution to the damp and soggy bits of our island home. Developments leaping forward, not to mention a remembering of ways past, are painting a picture of a new and exciting agricultural landscape.

What You Can Actually Chuffing Do:

Great Britain loves a curry – because we're only human and they're delicious. Have a crack at this cauliflower curry recipe and then send me abusive emails saying you want your lamb bhuna back – but *only* after you've actually tried it.

Cauliflower Jalfrezi Recipe – look, you know you want it

1 cauliflower

1 onion

1 yellow pepper

1 green chilli

1/2 jar jalfrezi spice paste

1 large potato

Big knob of ginger

3 cloves garlic

4 tomatoes

1 tin tomatoes

2 tsp sugar

Roast cauliflower in a light spray of oil and a generous sprinkling of garam masala for about 30 mins at 200 degrees until charred.

Chop onion into wedges and fry until soft, add chopped ginger, chilli and crushed garlic for the last minute or so. Add jalfrezi paste and fry for 2 mins. Add the potato in small cubes followed by the tomatoes. Add the tin of tomatoes and about 2/3 can of water. Bring to the boil and simmer until potatoes are nearly done. Add in pepper and sugar. Season. Stir in cauliflower.

Even better if made the day before. Serve with pilau rice. You're welcome.

Chapter 3
Guilt Trip: The Sequel

Unless you're an Instagram social influencer (shudder), chances are you tend to play down your privilege. Whilst those shiny, happy people whose income stream depends upon showing off and presenting a 'carefully curated' (is there a more loathsome phrase in English?) version of their lives (more commonly known as a lie) most people in the West are a little more humble about what they have. We all write our own narratives, just as much as we all like the smell of our own recycling bins.

Woman in the Mirror

People are very funny about accepting their own privilege. Not funny in a 'haha' way. Funny as in that person you used to work with making repeated attempts to add you on Facebook funny. Whenever people feel a little bit guilty about how they might have benefited from something, they have a tendency to bang on about being woke, snowflakes and cancel culture, but being aware of your own privilege as someone who's going to start caring more about the environmental crisis is important. It's also ok to not be perfect. It's ok to have not always been perfect – and because we're all infallible, to have dropped absolute clangers in the past. The awesome Maya Angelou always makes me feel better about things I have done/said/thought in the past: 'Do the best you can until you know better. Then when you know better, do better.' I love Angelou. Plus she makes it ok for us to still be learning, to be less entrenched and to live a gloriously uncurated existence. Phew.

Speaking of poetry, there is a rotten but somehow classically poetic irony with the running order of the *Climate Change Shitshow*. First up, naturally – because the universe has a wank sense of humour, the people who are going to be affected earliest and hardest are both the ones who have historically contributed the least to fucking our planet over *and* the people who the rich West will give the fewest fucks about. Neat. I accept that there's a limit on people's empathy for others – that's not sociopathic – it's a grinding reality of the world. If every single person in the UK was so torn up about child food poverty in their own country, county, town, they wouldn't be able to chuck out the contents of their soggy dew bins the night before their weekly shop. Life would be untenable. We'd feel like really shitty excuses for human beings all the time and I just do not have the energy/coffee for that. Extrapolate the compassion fatigue for people living in our own neighbourhoods to people from different cultures across vast geographical spaces and we give even less of a shit. It's exhausting: I'm meant to feel bad for the Bangaldeshis who are going to get flooded to shit, the Mauritians, same, the sub-Saharan farmers whose arable lands will turn to untillable dust, the displaced, the dispossessed and the needy? Oh, and I'm still meant to remember to put out grey bins this week and green the next? It would appear we all need to start training our badly out-of-shape compassion muscle. It seems to have been getting less and less action thanks to some pretty seedy grooming by capitalism and ruggedly individualistic ideologies.

Who says you're going to persuade me to do shit, Emma?

As a writer who cannot possibly imagine the life situations of the modest (potentially under duress) readership of this book, I am still willing to make some assumptions about the type of person you are. I'd wager you quite like your family (when they're not being dicks), you care about spending time with your friends, you enjoy bodily freedom, breathing clean air and food in your belly. You may be into *Minecraft* (dick), you may enjoy *Love Island* (who am I to judge?) or even *Bridgerton*, but I sincerely believe that most people aren't inherently dicks. For the most part, despite our differences and disparities, people just want to get on and live their lives, flex their kink, raise their families and bitch about their friends behind their backs. (Shut up, you know you do.) This is a privileged life and one many people around the globe cannot imagine being lucky enough to enjoy. The business of life is the living of it but there will be no life as we privileged few know it if we allow climate change to continue apace. Moreover, the poor bastards who would love to be able to be preoccupied with the shitty banalities of life in the wealthy West, will be the first to be fucked over by climate change and the least able to buy their way out of it. Dicks with super yachts don't need to worry – their staff will move their berth to a more hospitably-located marina. Dicks with multiple homes can choose to hole-up in the one in the most desirable climate. Dicks with underground bunkers will laugh in all of our faces, at least until they run out of fake tan. The climate emergency is going to shit all over humanity and, for the purposes of sensible discussion, we can exclude people with a metric chuff-tonne of money as they'll be fine; they're always fine.

It's the rest of us who need to worry. We also owe it to the people who have fuck all agency and who most of us don't give a shit about, not to make their lives any damn harder.

Get Geldof on the Blower

Our warming planet is getting increasingly biblical with every degree the mercury rises and, what's worse, there are not enough B-rate celebrities to help fundraise our way out of this one. We are going to see floods, storms, droughts, vast tracts of agricultural land becoming useless. Fires, tidal waves and probably plagues of locusts knowing our fucking luck. All pretty *Old Testament* levels of unpleasantness. Famine and resource scarcity will drive huge numbers of climate refugees which will probably lead to war because humans are just nice like that. The Red Cross estimates that in a six month period in 2020, 10.3 million people were displaced by climate related events. This is about four times the number displaced by war and conflict in the same period. But don't worry – if this trend continues, we'll have war and conflict caused by the displaced people because we lack empathy for others after about 5 minutes.

World's Greatest Endurance Event

I am good at enduring. Typically in a pretty stoic manner. I once managed to finish a cross country skiing expedition before admitting to having a bit of a gut ache. Peritonitis from a ruptured appendix as it turns out. I blame my grandmother for this. (The stoicism rather than the appendicitis.) When I was pregnant for the first time, I asked her what giving birth is like. As a single mother of five children – she should know. She said, without missing a beat, that, "it is a job of work." No Shit.

My husband would contend that I am a contrary little wotsit which is why I can just get on with it if I'm experiencing something hard/unpleasant/painful. (Coming from the redhead who ran six consecutive marathons across the Sahara Desert.) Conversely, although no less mentally taxing, I have been rained on *a lot* during my years working outdoors. One year it rained so much, my colleague got trench foot. Smells terrible, if you're wondering. Really terrible. There is a maxim that states, 'there's no such thing as bad weather – just bad clothing.' When people think of extreme weather they fail to conceptualise just how problematic this is becoming. Crops failing, rivers drying up and mass insect die-off are not mild inconveniences like the time you got soaked to the skin coming in from the shops. For millions of people around the world, there simply isn't the infrastructure to help them recover from 'a bit of weather.' The changing climate will be unendurable and, for many, unsurvivable.

Why do you care, Bear Grylls? You'll be laughing away with your survival mates in your little cave, chowing on some fresh venison.

Well, for starters, unless I'm very much mistaken, being able to knock out a few metres of nettle cordage (basically string) and forage for a few wild edibles isn't going to cut it when all the nettles are withered and…other people are bigger than me/have guns. Any 'preppers' who think they can ride it out remain (thankfully) utterly deluded. It doesn't matter how many vegetables you can grow yourself and how good at shelter-building you are. If we let the proverbial hit the fan, any resources an individual may have accrued will get robbed/you'll get stabbed unless you can employ a couple of heavies to protect you. But they probably eat a lot so such an endeavour may prove self-defeating.

Anorexia Riff

Anorexia riff was the working title for this section but I couldn't come up with anything funny to replace it with, so, here we are. There is a whole heap of dietary changes we need to get on board with if we stand a chance of limiting climate change to 1.5 degrees. For most of us, this dramatic shift from animal-based to plant-based will range from annoying to upsetting. I know how sincerely fucked off my kids are going to be when they find out I'm cancelling Fish Finger Friday and can picture the *exact* face my mother is going to pull when I tell her we're having a nut roast as the main event for Christmas dinner. Most people though, will have a few things to work through, a few family favourites to re-write and re-brand and they'll settle into a plant-based food culture without much trouble. Ironically, they'll be all the healthier for it as science (God, shut up science – such a dickwad!) categorically demonstrates that a plant-based diet is better for us *and* the planet – and *still* with the recalcitrance. Conversely, there are a group of people who are going to find this fucking difficult and perhaps even torturous and dangerous.

People who suffer from eating disorders will not find this transition easy. People who really like cheese (I'm so worryingly addicted – and I'm allowed to use that word because I read somewhere that it sets off the same brain receptors as Class A drugs which would go a long way to explaining how I repeatedly eat my bodyweight in the stuff every festive season) will probably somewhat lament having to break up with the Brie, but they'll look back and laugh about it at some point. This will not be the case for people with eating disorders. There's the famous adage about how alcoholics can give up drinking and, although it's apparently quite tricky, they can then say goodbye to their demon and enjoy recovery and a Diet Coke. People who have food as their demon, are not so lucky. They have to square-up to their demon three times a day, forever – until they die/climate change smokes them. That's pretty shit and people who have never battled with this particular nasty, would do well to not be a dick about it and show some compassion. Otherwise, my mother is coming at your legs with a slipper.

Speaking of Health

It is a truth universally acknowledged/said repeatedly by my mum, that without our health, we have nothing. Health is a privilege and as such, people who enjoy it, obviously take it totally for granted. Our warming climate is unequivocally harming human health. Already, the temperature increases are causing health problems in agricultural workers who have to undertake manual labour in extremely high temperatures, it is estimated by the WHO that air pollution (indoor and outdoor) kills 7 million people each year. This doesn't really sound ok to me. We all know how obsessed Brits are with knowing as much detail about the weather as possible but if you fancy freaking yourself out, DEFRA has an utterly terrifying daily pollution forecast and a postcode tool so you can see exactly what you, your family and pets are sucking in right now. At time of writing my babies are drinking down a 3. Anything above a 3 and 'adults and children with lung problems, and adults with heart problems' are advised not to undertake any strenuous activity outside. Guess that means the kids who have asthma can't enjoy break time at school then. Seems fair.

We kid ourselves that we can escape/evade/outrun climate change but according to the WHO, 99% of the world's population are living in places where their air quality guidelines aren't met. We are all breathing in the secondhand smoke of industry, transport, agriculture, Formula 1 racing driving (Why is no-one going after motorsport? It's entirely reliant on razzing through fossil fuels and treats women like decorations. WTF?) and we shouldn't be passively accepting of this. Air pollution is directly linked to asthma, other acute respiratory conditions, cancer, heart disease and stroke. I'll politely remind you that

I'd like to go quietly in my sleep, thank you very much. (Although hopefully not owing to a 'mercy pillow' from my kids who don't want to look after me any more/because I'm still wanging on about climate change.)

Rising temperatures really do a number on people's physical health and disproportionately affects the young, old and already vulnerable. Mental health also gets hammered when it's too hot. The summer I had my firstborn, we had a heatwave, when I was 9 months pregnant. Unless you have had a human exit your body, you do not get to tell me that this was 'just a bit of warm weather.' Rising temperatures also have an unhappy correlation with an increase in violent crime. This is a great deal more serious than you being a bit cranky with your spouse when they dare to breathe loudly during a hot summer night, but in the UK, we don't know the half of it. Pretty much literally. Global heat wave records continue to be broken in urban centres and cruelly, the only way to escape the heat is to crank the air conditioning even higher – in turn creating more emissions and thus warming the loo seat up for your grandkids.

Uncommon Sense

We all really need to stop aping Spoilt Brat Syndrome as modelled by much of Westminster. As we are all different, there will be different things that each of us can and can't do in order to contribute to slowing down our own destruction. A diabetic cannot give up the medical supplies wrapped in plastic needed to keep them alive, a builder specialising in eco-construction cannot stop driving their diesel van tomorrow, a hospital porter cannot give up commuting to work because it's too costly to live near their place of employment, a parent carer can't turn off their medically vulnerable child's equipment to save electricity. Petulant foot stomping along the lines of, "but I don't want to" needs to stop. Of course, we all want to enjoy ourselves but we are losing a sense of balance. We do not have a right to do 'anything' we want to because we enjoy it. Human appetites are not always a good indicator to make judgements on. Moreover, most of us are actually only afflicted with exceptionalism and entitlement.

Crank the Thermostat

Heating our homes is one of the biggest ecological challenges we face in the UK. This is because our climate specialises in cold and damp winter weather and our housing stock is more than a little shabby. It's perfectly possible to build 'passive' houses that lose almost no heat whatsoever through a little bit of clever engineering and planned services installation. It's really not sodding rocket science.

If it's so easy, why aren't all the new builds being built like this then, Emma?

In short, our old pals money and crappy regulatory edicts from the government. Sigh, sigh, sigh. It would be delightfully simple to just regulate that all new houses need to be built to stringent ecological standards and to begin the enormous undertaking of retrofitting, on a completely individualised basis, our existing housing stock – whilst bearing in mind that home insulation isn't necessarily the silver bullet we might like it to be.

Individual efforts are important – very much so and it's a shitty cop out to suggest that they make no difference. Moreover, I wouldn't hold my breath on our elected representatives doing *anything*, unbidden, that didn't directly benefit themselves. We need to 'motivate' them – preferably by being annoying and calling them out for broken promises. For example, our dearly beloved present Conservative government pledged (this means a solemn promise) at the 2019 General Election to plant an awful lot of trees. 30,000 hectares of trees, in fact, by 2024. I really hate to be the bearer of bad news, but they haven't done this. (This means they have lied.) At present, they're going at a rate of 1,260 hectares per annum – despite pledging to do 5,000 hectares each year. This inability to undertake even the most basic of climate mitigation strategies should not be rewarded by future votes. People's political disengagement is a completely logical and healthy response to the sideshow of Westminster, but we are going to have to pivot a little more towards active political engagement.

An Apple A Day

Tim Lang wrote that, 'the Department of Health has been aware for nearly two decades that diet-related non-communicable disease is helping bankrupt the NHS.' There is some very simple nutritional science that, if we choose to heed, can dramatically improve our own health, and that of the planet. More vegetables.

Special vegetables, coated in expensive nutritional powders and cooked over the embers of my dying love?

Nope. Just more veg. And fruit, but focus on the veg. It doesn't involve calorie counting, intermittent fasting, faecal transplants, 6 a.m. spin classes or giving up beer. Just eat more vegetables in place of animal products and highly processed crap, and you'll enjoy better health and a longer life. Well, not if you get run over carrying broccoli back from the greengrocers but otherwise, the advice is sound.

One of my besties has never eaten a banana. In fact, until he met his fiancée, I'm not sure he'd ever even (knowingly) eaten a vegetable. (I once gave him some courgette brownie, he didn't notice/complain.) Why are people so ambivalent about vegetables? We all happily guzzle roast potatoes and honey roasted peanuts (I swear they coat them in crack) but if someone offers you a serving of wilted cabbage or soggy carrots, it doesn't elicit quite the same excitement. At some point in British culinary history, some eejit declared that, 'it's not a proper meal' unless it's got meat in it. We are famous for meat and two veg – which seems a bit lacklustre compared to other food cultures, embarrassingly so.

I married a foreigner. He won't eat jelly *or* custard, saveloy, simnel cake, mushy peas, gherkins, vinegar on his chips, salad cream on anything and a multitude of other delicious items because he's weird/was raised in a different food culture. He was also a pretty stereotypical Australian meat lover. When I cooked fish (before I watched *Seaspiracy* and hated myself) I used to have to wrap the fillets in Parma ham so that he would be 'filled up.' He's actually pretty cool about how he was totally convinced of the animal protein myth and slightly embarrassed that when I first knew him, he would regularly eat an entire rotisserie chicken and a bag of Caesar salad (in a mixing bowl) because he 'needed' it for muscle recovery after training. After some gentle nagging/relentless ear bashing he now concedes that vegetables are awesome and all 6'3" of him quite happily and healthily exists without animal protein. He also demonstrates that you can change your household's food culture. Previously, my husband said that he'd, "rather eat dog shit than lentils" (his words). Recently, I was away for a few days and he ate dal bhat (Nepalese lentils and rice) for five consecutive dinners.

At present, my household enjoys a lot of Mexican (ish, properly speaking probably Tex Mex), Indian, Nepalese (if you haven't tried momos, you need to), Italian and plenty of 'traditional British' favourites but steering well clear of trying to recreate meat and two (limp, overcooked) veg. British food culture is rich and tasty (despite its humble origins and international derision) but has not been enhanced by buckets of greasy chicken wings and beef patties in sweaty buns. So, why the hell are we all so hooked? Convenience, speed, proliferation, whopping (see what I did there) marketing budgets and the unholy trifecta of salt, fat and sugar have a lot to answer for. The down right ubiquity also makes it really hard to avoid these eateries that treat its suppliers, staff and customers in a uniformly cruddy manner. These food giants wield an awful lot of power, and this hegemony must be challenged if we are to save stuff/the planet/each other.

The Poacher turned Gamekeeper

Now I don't know about you, but I wasn't exactly very useful to the Covid cause during the pandemic. Sure, I gave my mate some loo roll when he ran out because Brits are unceasingly weird about toileting, but being useless at proper science meant I was out of the running for being useful to the brilliant (and kind) Chris Whitty, JvT *et al.*

Hang on, this whole book has been about science and you're now admitting your lack of qualifications?

Shhh, pet. It's not like Gove had anything useful to add to the education sector but that never held him back. So, as I said, I haven't been very helpful during the pandemic (or, indeed, ever) but there is something marvellous that anyone can do – whether you're a clever science boffin or not…take some personal responsibility for screwing up the planet a bit less. Stop passing the buck/patiently waiting for central government to hand you a solution that means your life can magically continue exactly as it is whilst the planet recuperates – those beans are not going to be forthcoming.

Far be it for me to sound ungrateful, but the pandemic hasn't been great environmentally speaking. Sure, it was great when no one was flying or driving to the office daily and we were all having to make do with sphagnum moss for bog roll (I'm looking at you, sodding hoarders) but that has pretty much fallen by the wayside. Moreover, personal car use is actually higher than pre-pandemic levels as people try to avoid getting the plague from being crammed onto packed tube trains. Also, and legitimately so, the pandemic has increased and revived a lot of single-use product waste. Masks (proper ones – not like my one with a Harry Potter lightning scar on it), PPE, medical supplies, LFD testing and so on contain a lot of non-recyclable single use material. For now, there's not a whole heap we can do about this.

Charlton Heston drawling that there was, "no more precious inheritance," (than the right to bear arms) 15 seconds after a load of children were massacred in their school is something that we pretty unanimously agree is in poor taste. What is also in poor taste is people banging their drums about medical waste and hospitals. Imagine for a moment that you yourself have a chronic medical condition, or that you're a parent carer for a medically vulnerable child. What you really wouldn't need is people making you feel bad about plastic medical waste – not least because there are bigger and vastly more culpable fish to fry. Sterile medical equipment is not something we should be looking to retire – it's literally life-saving equipment and there are many more fruitful waste-reduction avenues we can be pursuing. So, we can't change the course of the waste produced by the pandemic but there's a lot we can do about what we shove in our gobs. Plenty. 15% of all global emissions are directly linked to animal husbandry. Imagine if we were *only* having to deal with the other 85% of the mess we made.

Books are a Gateway Drug

As a child and being contrary, I was both resolutely bookish (girly swot) and an avid outdoors person (muddy tomboy – because it was the 1980s and we all really struggled with traditional ideas of femininity). I'm pleased to inform you, dear reader, that not much has changed – I enjoy nature and cutting nature down to turn it into books. Fortunately, when I was a teenager you were meant to be unattractive and awkward so I felt no shame in getting the bus straight from school to go to the library in my local town. There I would happily wander the aisles, slyly choosing the Judy Blumes with the sexy bits in them and pairing them with botanical volumes and adventure stories – variety is the spice of life. Arthur Ransome inspired me with a love for the natural world and whilst he's indirectly responsible for me dislocating a kneecap halfway down Great Gable, I don't begrudge him an ounce. Slightly more questionable is his handling of Northerners and depictions of people from China, but he was a dude, so he's *allowed* to be complex. Moreover, at the risk of sounding patronising, good nature writing can bring to life something that just isn't accessible to all people. Non-disabled people take for granted the ability to trudge up Snowdon on a rainy day or delighting in choosing *not to* trudge up Snowdon on a rainy day. If you have mobility issues (that's what the Queen had, she didn't do 'old'), are old, disabled or in anything less than in tip top cardiovascular health, the 3 Peaks Challenge is likely off-limits to you. The best nature writing, both fiction and non-fiction, acts as a window for those who can't be there in person. There is an important caveat that needs to be noted here – plenty of jolly, wholesome children's adventure stories contain thoroughly racist, colonial and sexist language, ideas and assumptions. There are different opinions on how to broach this with children and even Disney who have plenty of dollars to spend on inclusivity advisers struggled to find the words for this chat. I think it's good to point out to children the language choices and that the ideas that informed them sucked and still suck. Tempting as it is to skip over the repeated, racist rants about the 'Indians' (Native Americans) Ma seemingly so enjoys in *Little House on the Prairie*, we probably won't be doing the youth any favours until we can freely admit that white people have a lot to answer for.

Tell me you didn't?

I did. Sorry, not sorry. And enough with the pearl-clutching over Critical Racial Theory education, already. Look at Germany's example of reparation and restitution after the Second World War. Once more for the thickos at the back: We. Must. Learn. From. The. Past. Which. We. Cannot. Do. Unless. We. Talk. About. It.

God, I would have hated you if you were my teacher.

When I was teaching you friction firelighting or dragging you through a compulsory War Poetry module? Just out of interest.

Anyway, we don't all need to be into nature in the super nerdy manner that I am, but we all need to show at least a passing interest. This means engaging, involving and listening to a wider swathe of society, making it a compulsory component of schooling so that we get the next generation of nerdy nature scientists all fired up, ready to invent something really clever to clean up this big old mess we created for them.

Pleasingly, there is a new GCSE being introduced on Natural History which, whilst not precisely addressing and redressing the Eurocentric, outdated curriculum which teachers gut themselves trying to get their students through, is a start. Minimal gains and all that.

Representations of the Wild Places

The outdoors education industry in the UK, although not exactly singular in this respect, is predominantly run and staffed by white men. When I applied for a job at a well-known company, there were 16 men and me at our selection process/interview. (Thank you, equal opportunities.) Having seen the clientele of the industry, this isn't because they were fiendishly sexist, but rather that I was probably the only girl who applied. Over the course of my time working for them, there were a grand total of three women out of a field team running at about 30. My boss being a well-known personality, I also had to regularly endure being asked when at an RV point to collect clients, whether I was his secretary. Now, my information on this score may be a little bit out of date because I haven't done any residential outdoor education work since I had my babies. But I suspect that rather proves my point...

Overwhelmingly, outdoors education professionals are white men. And whilst there's nothing inherently pernicious with this *per se*, this creates two issues: the first being that it perpetuates the idea that nature and wildlife in the UK is 'something for white people.' Imagine your typical rambler/National Trust member/climbing instructor...see, white man. The second issue is that people are unlikely to show an interest in a subject if they feel it's 'not for them' or not welcoming to them. I'm of the opinion that this in turn, means that discussions regarding the environment totally exclude important stakeholders – by which I mean an actually, realistic representation of the society we live in. (And, incidentally, are trying to save in case you're still getting up to speed.) Britain has a proud tradition of 'controlling the narrative,' also known as 'making sure we come out sounding good.' For example we all know that it was William Wilberforce who campaigned to end slavery while we ignore the contributions (at much greater personal cost) of people such as Olaudah Equiano and Mary Prince. There has been some brilliant work done by people other than old, white dudes on ecological writing, but you don't need to skip ahead to my Suggested Reading List to guess that the majority of widely-read books on the ecological crisis are by, drum roll…white dudes. The inherent biases in academic fields are well documented and consistently show that it's basically shit trying to be a woman or LGBTQ+ person in science. The trickle-down effect is that there are far fewer non-white-male perspectives available to purchase on Amazon when you're tipsy, and this matters.

Urgh, stop trying to be so woke, Emma.

What even is *woke*? It's one of those insults that feels as though someone is slagging you off for feeling empathy for others. Or someone who's enjoyed a shit-tonne of privilege liking to believe that they made it through virtue of their character and hard work.

Let's get back to fixing this mess.

What You Can Actually Chuffing Do:

1. Stop ironing. Dead simple and you'll save about 800g of carbon dioxide for each hour of your life you don't spend smoothing clothes that are imminently going to get unsmoothed. What a win.
2. Use a washing line/airer rather than a tumble drier. Your electricity bill will thank you.
3. Wash your clothes less frequently.
4. Breeders – use cloth nappies, cool wash, air dry.
5. Don't charge your phone overnight.
6. Switch to an eco-friendly internet browser. Yes, such things exist, I use Ecosia.
7. Delete old emails – server storage space uses energy and you are *never* re-reading them.
8. Make reusable 'wet wipes'/kitchen paper/rags out of old t-shirts. Cool wash, air dry.
9. Switch energy providers to one that uses more renewable energy.
10. Beware the Greenwash Monster – be annoying and ask questions.

Chapter 4
It's Cool to be a Dick

Chances are, unless you really like the word dick (me too, great minds) you are probably reading this book because somewhere, lurking at the back of your mind, you're becoming increasingly conscious that, just maybe, science is something we ought to be heeding in regards to the certain demise of our one and only home. Perhaps you are vegan-curious – ok, well not curious because it sounds like a totally joyless existence where you can't even have cheese, but perhaps you're feeling bad every time you throw your plastic coffee cup into the polar bear enclosure at the zoo…Whatever your motivation, it's hard to argue with Chris Goodall who says that, 'if you have decided not to fly, moving to a plant-based diet is possibly the single most important action you can take next.' And of course you've decided not to fly as much as is humanly possible as you wouldn't want to be one of the 15% of the population who makes 70% of all flights. Because that might make you a dick.

Insufferable Know-it-alls

Remember when Emma Watson gave that illustrative example that put to bed forever the assertion that only certain sorts of people are feminists? Hairy, angry, bra-burning etc. – you know, those fun tropes. Well, here's the thing if you like any of the following, guess what, you're a feminist, I mean dick/eco-warrior.

Do you care about:

Polar bears?

Access to fairly-priced and healthy food?

Access to any food?

Women's reproductive and educational rights?

Habitable homes for all people on Earth?

Well whoop-de-fucking-do – you're a climate non-dick. Less catchy than it could be but I'm working on it.

Swear on the *Bible*

I don't doubt that you were hoping I'd left my doom-mongering in Chapter 1 so we could spend the remainder of the book cussing and feeling superior. But I need to make you aware of a couple of things. Firstly, they are now able to produce wine in Norway. Oh dritt. Norway, the country famed for having to eat tinned potatoes and Ratfisk because it's too bloody cold to grow anything else.

What's Ratfisk?

It's a Norwegian 'delicacy' and even Norwegians would sheepishly admit that they are taking a liberty with that term. It's a fish they catch and allow to ferment/decompose/rot a bit, sometimes they bury it under the ground for up to a year, they dig it up and obviously don't cook it before eating it.

Like smoked salmon? That's called curing you philistine.

Nope, it's called rotting – it certainly smells like rotting. Regrettably, I have firsthand experience of being exposed to this stuff and, nope, no thank you, no sirree.

Once again, my lack of expertise is showing but I thought wine regions were meant to be warm and sunny unless…oh no – we've messed things up so much they're planting vines on the old cross-country ski routes. Ratfisk indeed.

Shithole Countries

As our dearly beloved Donnie let slip, behind closed doors, world leaders don't pussyfoot around discussing less economically developed countries, predominantly agrarian societies and the like. They've got countries to run and as such are time poor. It's much quicker to divide the world up into Shithole Countries (SCs) and Not Shithole Countries (NSCs). There is quite a range of unpleasantness to be found in the SCs, for example, malaria, ebola, drought, famine, unrest caused by water and food insecurity. To Trump's (miniscule) mind, SCs were mostly in Africa but he also gave

Haiti a special mention. What everyone could agree with was that he meant countries with a mostly black or brown population and we can also agree that he figures we don't need to trouble ourselves too much with them and their silly insistence on climate driven crop failure, infrastructural limitations and mass migration. But fear not, Mother Nature is fierce and really doesn't like Trust Fund Bellends (TFBs) – she has the matter in hand. In some of the modelling done by the London School of Hygiene and Tropical Medicine (which always makes me think they're good at dealing with horrendous spider bites but also shower daily) it's forecast that by 2078, nearly 90% of the Earth's population would be at risk of catching malaria and a separate study estimates that disease-carrying mosquitoes could be established in Europe by 2030. And the diseases they enjoy carrying are zika, yellow fever, dengue, kala-azar, chikungunya (yeah, I had to look that one up too) as well as malaria. All bad, all unpleasant at best, fatal at worst.

I thought you said we were killing off all the insects?

Only the good ones it seems.

Is there never *a bright side to climate change?*

Seven Plagues for Seven Bloggers

In the *Bible*, Egypt suffered 10 plagues (omnipotence means he knew decimalisation was coming) because everyone was being a dick and refusing to free the Israelite slaves. One of them was locusts. (The plagues, not the Israelites.) Locusts or grasshoppers come in a few incarnations across the globe, but the headlines are they're great at breeding, like really big parties and will eat everything they swarm across. As per the *Bible*, this is good at triggering food insecurity, famine and migration because there's nothing left to harvest once they've been through town. It is the very worst sort of stag weekend in Prague where the participants ate everything they touched for three days, before impregnating all the local women with clones of their town-wrecking selves to pop out next time some drunk bloke has a slash up against a public memorial. Lads, lads, lads. Over the last few years, the Horn of Africa has taken a real battering from desert locusts (*Schistocerca gregaria*) and at present they cause the greatest harm to subsistence farming regions of Africa. Recent shifts to heavy rain events which saturate the land and make for ideal locust breeding and swarming events are attributed to climate change and with such trends forecast to continue and potentially worsen, more communities and their food supplies are going to be at risk from this insect. Very grievous, indeed.

With changing rain patterns and warmer temperatures our old biblical pal the plague of locusts might visit people in NSCs. A swarm of 30-40 million desert locusts (the ones with particularly hearty appetites) can eat the same amount of food in a single day as 35,000 people. They also create a cascade of ecological harms – by eating all the vegetation, local temperatures increase, impacting water supplies and the ability of the land and communities to recover.

Not on my allotment.

That's the point though – even if we aren't that bothered when all the food is gone from Kenya, South Sudan and Uganda, we might be a bit more upset when we have no oats, no wheat, no medicinal opium. All I'm saying is that we've had a plague, NSW, Australia got the (most publicised) floods (they were much, much worse in Durban, South Africa, but you know, brown and black people) and locusts might well be next on the terrifyingly biblical menu.

Only the Good Insects Die Young

Conversely, *A Bug's Life* risks becoming a period piece. The rate of climate-induced extinction in insects is eight times faster than the rate at which we are killing birds, mammals and reptiles. We unknowingly depend on insects a lot. Not just the ones with the proficient press officers like ladybirds (aphid-munchers), worms (nutrient recyclers and soil savers) and spiders (so my house isn't overrun with flies). They are critical to the ecological health of our planet. They do an awful lot of work behind the scenes to enable us to have food to eat thanks to them pollinating it, providing food for other animals and recycling nutrients so we can eventually consume them. (The nutrients not the insects, although, more on bug munching later.) I also feel we might need to get past the Janet Jackson approach to the environment…

What Have You Done for Me Lately?

Insects, plants and animals shouldn't have to *justify* their existence by being 'useful members of society'/the ecosystem. We are attempting to apply capitalist principles. (Which we can all agree, are pretty sketchy – a reminder that in 2017 Oxfam's wealth report showed that the eight richest people on Earth have as much money as the poorest half of humanity. That's around 3.7 billion people having the same, combined, as eight *really* rich twats.) Every single species should have the basic right to exist and before anyone gets silly, I'm obviously not championing horrible flesh-eating microorganisms, and besides, Russia has plenty of these preserved for super unsubtle assassinations. We are not supposed to be judge, jury and executioner for which species get to survive. The last time we tried that, the poor bloke was so overworked from boat building and list making, he couldn't even remember his wife's name.

You Can't Still Feel the Butterflies: They're Dead

So, if we look past the critical but unlovable insect losses, what about the decorative ones? Butterflies in Britain declined by 58% on farmed land in less than a decade. And we all know how pretty they are. Moths are the mousy younger sister to the popular butterfly, but these nighttime treasures are no less precious. Sadly, bumblebee numbers are also declining, and I have a bit of a thing for bumblebees. Maybe it's the fur talking, but they are just so cute and industrious, they tend to steal the show. We must remember that there are around 270 British bee species, at the moment anyway, but bees are really doing battle. They are fighting a loss of habitat, extreme weather and shifting seasonal patterns, parasites, diseases (many of which are exacerbated by warming temperatures), invasive species and pesticides. Speaking of invasive species, the Asian hornet (*Vespa velutina*) is not meant to live in Europe and our native species are not equipped to cope with being eaten by it. It's predominantly the honey bee who the hornets find so delicious but should the Asian hornet really get established, it's a bit of a red squirrel scenario.

Thiamethoxam – Lord of the Bee Killers

Sugar has a pretty terrible track record. It rots our teeth, makes us fat and was a key part of the slave trade. Modern sugar companies are understandably keen to distance themselves from such unpleasantness, but they aren't as saccharine as they'd have you believe. British Sugar lobbied (you just know this is going to end well) for the use of a banned pesticide that all ecologists agree is ferociously harmful to nature. Big Sugar likes to invoke the 'poor farmer' motif at this point but what they really mean is 'poor shareholders.' Individual farmers in areas affected by yellow virus could easily be supported through a bad sugar beet harvest if their employers weren't quite so concerned about bulging profit margins. 'We look after our farmers, as long as they don't need looking after.' Smells like capitalism alright. Scientists didn't push for a ban on this group of pesticides (the neonicotinoid ones) because they are prone to hysteria. In fact, show me a demographic less prone to irrational outbursts. This stuff is bad and is especially harmful to bees – who we really, really need to look after as they are prolific pollinators and without pollination, WE WILL HAVE NOTHING TO EAT. This is obviously worse than us having a bit less sugar to eat for a couple of harvests, in affected areas. It also damages waterways because most of the pesticides, whether they are initially sprayed on plants in the fields or used to coat the seeds, end up washing into the water table and finding their way to the ocean. Also, if we focused our attention a bit harder on trying to arrest rising global temperatures, we wouldn't be providing the very conditions such pests need to thrive and proliferate. It feels a bit like someone complaining they're got a sore throat and you cutting the heads off everyone in a 5 mile radius to 'treat' it. If you still need convincing, note that it is estimated that it would cost around £1.8 billion per year for farmers to manually pollinate the crops. And thanks to the

Ministry of Brexit Opportunities, we are a bit short of willing farm hands.

The Other White Meat

I have eaten a few insects in my time. Some intentionally. I once woke up in the woods (always with the light and birdsong, so smug) and thought that I'd been dribbling as I slept. My rolled up jumper/pillow was a bit wet and slimy too and there was a trail of dribble from the corner of my mouth, into my hair. It was slug slime, as it turns out. For the record, slugs taste bad.

Different cultures are ok with eating different things. Plenty of people eat insects around the world as a nutritious and delicious source of protein.

I thought we were meant to be saving the insects, Emma, not eating them?

Well, yes and no. We need to protect as best we can insects in the wild, but farming insects is a different and very sensible proposition. It's much more sustainable because it uses far fewer resources than conventional animal husbandry and still lets us get that important protein fix – everyone's suddenly a nutritionist once you start talking about giving up meat. Insects are really good from a nutritional standpoint, in that they contain lots of nutrients, amino acids and protein. They are also really good from an environmental standpoint. They use less water and food to rear and emit fewer greenhouse gases. Their bodily waste to yield ratio is great too – pretty much 100% whereas with cows, only 40% of the animal is consumable. For the purpose of research, I ate my way through a selection box of different flavour cricket snack bags. They were really delicious; I would gladly eat them again and my kids snarfed them with their typical culinary discernment. One did get dropped though and my dog ate it, and promptly spat it back out. So, I guess we're not switching her from her chicken kibble to an insect based one. Just in case you needed further prodding, the marketing material for one UK based company claims that: to obtain 1kg of protein from cows, 2,850g of greenhouse gases are emitted, 22,000 litres of water, 10,000g of feed and 200 square metres of cultivable land are needed as opposed to crickets which emit 1g of greenhouse gases, require 1 litre of water, 1,700g of feed and 15 square metres of cultivable land. Those are some pretty sexy exoskeletal figures.

There is a caveat though: insects have been found to be capable of feeling pain. The way they are typically processed is through freezing or macerating so we're potentially back at the chick in a blender thing (more on this later) which we may wish to avoid. Also, the scale of insect farming is far greater – you can get a lot more Mopane worms (*Gonimbrasia belina*) on a farm than cows and generational cycles are much shorter. Thus, we are potentially inflicting a phenomenal amount of suffering on mind-boggling numbers of creatures and maybe this ought to be a consideration. Because mankind's Karma score sheet is in even worse health than The Great Barrier Reef.

Protein Low Down

The British Heart Foundation has suggested that it's healthier to get most of our protein from plant-based sources – thus extending your life and that of the planet. Adults need around 50g of protein a day and in the UK, most adults tend to eat double what they actually require a day – because we literally don't do things by halves. The protein myth is a pervasive one and people like to cling really hard to it when feeling defensive about meat eating. But it is just that – a myth. You can be perfectly healthy eating a plant-based diet – and you can also be perfectly unhealthy subsisting on meat-replacement products and chips. (These vegans exist but are just less popular on Instagram.)

The Woman who made Water in the Woods

When I lived in the woods…

Oh, here we go again

…much of my time was consumed by meeting my immediate needs. Water, shelter, fire, food. There is a simple satisfaction to being able to see the very direct results of your labours – far more satisfying than any type of work I have found since.

cough cough

Apart from writing this book – *obviously* this fills my heart with gladness.

You were saying…?

I had a few different options for how to source water. Often, we had an agreement with a nice local farmer who would let us fill 20 litre jerry cans before having to do my best *World's Strongest 5'3", 8 Stone Wet Through, But I'm Not Asking For Help, Woman* impression and walk, teeth gritted, using the joyful 'farmer's walk,' back to our camp. This wasn't always an option though but fortunately, Britain's (presently) temperate climate has your back.

If you need water (and you do, approximately 3 litres per day) and there isn't a running stream or open body of water in close proximity, but you stumble across some boggy ground you're in luck. You just have to dig yourself a gypsy well (a *Traveller* well?) to get yourself a drink.

Living outdoors seems to involve a lot of digging.

You simply need to dig yourself a decent hole and wait until it fills with water – this seeping isn't very speedy but once you've done that, you bail out the water as the first lot is a muddy slop, and let it refill and then, taking a Millbank bag (looks like an old fashioned sock) you scoop up the cleanest water you can manage, hang the bag on a branch over a billy can, and watch it drip through the designated seam one drop at a time, as the dense cotton fabric filters out the heavy particulate matter. This takes a really, really long time. Once you have enough water to make a brew, you light a fire, hang the billy on the pot holder you've engineered while you were waiting and bring the water to a rolling boil to kill the microorganisms that make you poorly/shit yourself a lot. In theory, the water is then safe. Unless there's *Giardia* in the water system (a very nasty parasite) or agricultural run-off in the form of fertiliser, pesticide or animal waste – all of which will make you pretty crook. All things being equal, you've just made the world's best cup of tea. This process – several hours of work – is far removed from an instant purchase of a £1.80 plastic bottle of water the second you step off the tube because you're a bit thirsty, but it demonstrates just how broken our relationship with water consumption is.

Big Drips

We leave taps running and dripping, luxuriate in long showers and top up our baths with more hot water so we can finish the next chapter of our amusing books on ecology. We demonstrably take water for granted. Water is essential to our daily life on Earth and yet most of us wouldn't know what to do 12 hours after the taps ran dry. Huge infrastructure disruption is a likely consequence of climate events and the more events we allow to happen, the more it won't be possible to recover from the last punch, before the next one is landed. In addition, water scarcity (even in rainy places like Britain) is increasingly prevalent and really, it's not ok that the Moroccan farm labourers are getting kidney stones from dehydration while the strawberries we insist on eating year-round are plump and juicy from the irrigation systems bleeding local water resources dry.

Come Early, Bring Lentils

So, what does a less ecologically damaging life look like? Different – that's for sure. Really, really different. There are small, personal actions that are important to make and particularly useful for virtue-signalling and feeling fucking smug at your next family get-together/Whatsapp argument. We are all familiar with being encouraged to use less plastic, take a train somewhere in Europe rather than flying and eating fewer animal products. These are all great, but there is a bigger dick issue we need to tackle…

I studied Politics at A-Level. Yeah – even my 16-year-old self was cool. I could not, in my wildest imaginings, have believed that someone who insisted on a cameo in *Home Alone 2* so the production could shoot in the hotel he bought with Daddy's money, would ever get elected to the highest office in America and one of the most influential seats of power on Earth. I could have guessed that he liked grabbing women by their genitals because I can spot a dick at 100 paces. Nor could I have imagined that the British public would elect a journalist who slagged off (brown) people for their (non-Christian) religion and stirs up xenophobia to leave a political union that was established to bring stability and unity. There is a worrying trend here – these dickheads didn't seize power in a violent coup – they were *elected*. I feel as though the UK and US in particular need to stick up some fucking massive post-it notes that say, 'Stop electing bellends who give zero shits about anyone but themselves.' Seriously, don't give a vote to someone who is a dick or who supports (or even fails to oppose) dick-policies. What's a dick policy? Glad you asked. They are political policies that don't see children as deserving of a full belly when they lay in bed at night. Policies that still, despite them LITERALLY SAVING OUR FUCKING ARSES IN THE PANDEMIC, don't pay healthcare staff a fair wage.

We need better leaders – we need to *elect* better leaders. Stop voting for dicks because your family always have/you don't like the other one/don't trust women/people of colour/the Tories will at least look after the economy. Vote for people and parties that at least *pretend* to give a shit. And if they renege on their whimsical campaigning promises, vote their lying, lazy arses out the second that you can. Individual choices that impact the environment are really, really good but on their own, won't change the rate at which we are screwing over our planet. We need political will and action to scale up the rate of change by a really big factor. (One I could guess at had I had more interest in maths at school, but you know, a lot.) Also, as much as it pains me to say it, we need to send more good people into the viper's nest. We need to start diluting the cronyism with some people with better ethics.

"Mummy, I'd like to enter politics when I grow up."

"Are you sure you wouldn't like to give sex work a go, poppet?"

Perhaps I'm being hysterical unnecessarily, but I want my children to be good and do good, not be corruptible and do their parliamentary researcher. Call me a Tiger Mummy, if you will.

Big Dick Energy

Why is it that lots of really good people are still struggling so profoundly to 'get on the planet-saving train?' I'm no psychologist but I have a hunch that it's the absurd enormity of the task at hand. Like, what the actual fuck? We've done so much damage to the only place we can live (shut up Elon, we really need to be practical at this point) that it may already be too late to preserve the way of life we really enjoy? We are all being stupid fucking ostriches right now. This problem is so big, it doesn't matter if I consume so much coffee that I can see through walls – I just cannot conceive of it.

Given the potential futility of affecting meaningful change – what's the sodding point? There isn't an easy, honest answer to this. This makes me so sad I almost can't breathe and, hello anxiety for my babies and what a clusterfuck I'm leaving for them to wade through.

However, we have to retain hope. How? Er, pass, but I know that it's really important that we do. It's going to be difficult enough to stop the worst ever disaster movie from playing out in real time but kicking arses and taking names will be a great deal more challenging if we don't come at it with a decent expectation of being successful.

So, you want us to switch from pretending that climate change isn't a problem to pretending it's a massive problem but a solvable one, even when it potentially isn't? You're insane.

In essence yes and no; giving up means certain death for everyone and everything I like – I'd like to give it my best shot.

I'm not the only one in a bit of a muddle. Wildlife regulations and natural world policies aren't always the most current or coherent. For example, under the 1992 Badger Protection Act, it is an offence to wilfully kill, injure or steal a badger. (You know that clause is in there because someone, somewhere robbed a badger. Hero.) Equally, and arguably bafflingly, it's possible to get a licence to cull badgers in an attempt to curb the spread of bovine tuberculosis. This strategy has been controversial (you think?) and ineffective – moreover, it sounds a touch conflicted. Perhaps if we weren't eating cows, we wouldn't feel so justified in culling an ancient, native species for potentially impacting our stream of steaks.

There are too many issues for me to keep track of Emma.

There really are and I haven't even mentioned salmon farming, peatland degradation, the demise of keystone species...

Vegans *Literally* Can't Eat Anything

One of the ugly accusations 'some' people (probably dicks) have levelled at veganism is that it's too fucking extreme.

Yeah, chill out and have a cheese toastie already.

"Look, I love animals too, lambs are just so fluffy and cute but I think vegans just take the whole thing too far." This is the sort of thing nice people say about vegans (behind their backs) but a lot of people have been turned off by what is regarded as the radical nature of veganism and this really is the fault of vegans.

Thank God we're finally back to bashing vegans; I'm relieved.

A lot of vegans have not helped the cause by lecturing (*ad nauseam*) all the normal, animal-scoffing innocent people in their lives about how bad they were (yawn) and how they're killing the planet and themselves and they should [SUBJECT CHANGE] because we all know that nothing kills a buzz or spoils Christmas as quickly as a vegan on a soap box/at your dinner table.

However, because we broke our planet, it's time for people/dicks to stop calling vegans dicks and *shudder* start listening to what they have to say. Yes, they're annoying and some of them are still twats but they kind of have a point – a very salient one, as it happens.

If animal protein were invented now, we'd ban it. Ok, that analogy works a lot better with alcohol but I'm lightheaded from all the swearing. Cruelty to another species because we've been doing it since forever/the advent of battery farming in the 1960s isn't a morally defensible position. Almost all meat we eat in the UK comes from the global factory system which takes baby cows away from their mummies, burns chicken's beaks off (no anaesthesia), cuts pigs' bollocks off (still no anaesthesia) and these are the welfare-certified farms. Modern meat and dairy has gritty origins – something we deliberately avoid knowing too much about. We all avoid thinking too closely about the process of fluffy chick to drumstick in a bucket because it would put us off our fucking bucket of chicken (duh!). It has only recently occurred to me that this is conceptually weird. Buckets are great for measuring cement and quantities of rain but maybe we shouldn't be buying avian flesh by the *bucket*. Just a thought.

It Clucks to be a Chicken

We consume almost a billion chickens a year in the UK. The British Poultry Council says that chicken is eaten on 6.3 billion occasions annually and the 95% of the British population who eat chicken tend to do so twice a week. Here's another dietary quirk – most people in the UK have reduced their consumption of red meat which is, theoretically, positive. Mad cow disease probably has a legacy in this instance as well as people regarding red meat as potentially injurious to health. Chicken though – pass me the bucket of drumsticks – is another balls up. We are all supposed to be eating less meat – not more of a different sort. Perhaps we ought to remind ourselves that chickens are still living creatures and not somehow less bothered than cows, pigs and sheep about being dinner.

Cheeky Libel Case?

Nando's is a Portugese-ish (confident they're not claiming to be that authentic) restaurant chain that has achieved cult status amongst young diners in Britain. Its success has been meteoric and dining there often features a good, old fashioned 'spice off' where men prove their virility and *#metoo* alliance by trying to order the spiciest sauce with their mass-produced chicken. Lads, lads, lads.

Chickens are funny birds and have a lot of spunk for something that will be slaughtered at around 6 weeks old. Some only manage 28 days to point of kill which sounds monumentally rubbish.

At least they're running around oblivious until they are packed off for dispatching.

Many 'broiler' chickens actually can't run for shit because we breed our meat chooks to be so huge their skeletons can't cope, and if we breed them for eggs, many of them spend their lives confined in a shit-spattered crate popping out egg after egg. Where was I? Yeah, so chickens get used for meat and eggs but they're not actually the same breed and a few years ago we all got upset about battery hens and there has been a big shift towards 'free range' laying hens but free range is a very loose term and it really isn't as wholesome as it sounds. More about marketing labels and industry standards later. The chickens we eat in the UK don't have a very nice life. 95% of them are grown indoors in industrial warehouses. Some of the practices used routinely in the industry include burning the ends of little chicks' beaks off and macerating unwanted boy chicks. If you need a mental image for this, this is putting live chicks in a blender and turning it on: *cheep cheep.*

Nando's has tapped into our insatiable appetite for cheap animal protein. You can no more check the provenance of your chicken blathered in piri-piri than I can identify whatever the hell my toddler found on the floor of the bathroom and has already swallowed. There are, in reality, only a minuscule number of people raising meat in the UK in a vaguely nice way and this isn't because our farmers are monsters, but because the big supermarkets and multinational fast food outlets drive a stupidly hard bargain and most of us don't shop/eat anywhere else. Cheap food has seduced those of us with cash and entrapped those without. Maybe we could ask the bellends in government (any bellend will do) why, when food is at a historically low price relative to income, we still have such widespread food poverty in the UK. They'll get back to you the moment they return from their Club, I'm sure. (Chippy, moi?)

At least we can still eat fish, right?

Unless you've been living under a rock, you probably know that our oceans are in every bit as much peril as our *terra firma*.

Yes, but farmed fish isn't touching the wild stocks; surely that's ok?

Salmon farming isn't any prettier up close than an intensive industrial scale chicken shed. Sea lice infestations are common and sometimes they're so bad, the critters are eating the salmon alive. Chemical usage in salmon farming in the UK increased by over 1000% 2005-2015 so it's not quite as 'natural' and healthy as you might be inclined/lead by aggressive marketing to believe. Salmon farms in particular generate a lot of fish shit in a concentrated area and a reminder, that we should and need to feel an affinity with all living beings; salmon farming isn't very nice if you're a salmon. Just because salmon won't do tricks for us or flop onto our paddle boards for a belly rub, doesn't mean they are any less deserving of humane treatment.

Those Videos

We've all seen those mad vegan dicks on the High Street with their leaflets 'Meat is Murder' (activists just *love* alliteration) and in recent times, when we'd all gotten bored of watching *Tiger King*, people's attention has turned to *Cow/Sea/Meat is Badspriacy* documentaries. These programmes contained some pretty mild footage in all honesty and yet I still feel like I need to wash my retinas after watching those darling baby whales getting slaughtered with their mummies. Sob.

I once had a housemate who wouldn't buy chicken if there was 'red' on it. I didn't mention what I did for a living. Is there any excuse for *not* watching videos of supermarket chickens living a horrible life and enduring a bad death? What morality can we claim to have if scenes of suffering – be it people or livestock – do not impact us and make us want to stop the suffering? If I went for a stroll around a kill floor at an abattoir, I'd probably have nightmares for weeks. What trauma must this be inflicting on the workers? They cannot look away as we do.

Shall I just be straight with you?

Most of us are going to need to give up meat. Entirely. Hell, maybe I should be totally up front. Most of us are going to need to be a dick/vegan and give up dairy products too. The thing is, you see, (I'm stalling), that, well, even if you give up beef, by consuming dairy, you're still contributing to a hell of a lot of cow farts (methane is really bad, remember) the razing of the rainforests for the growing of soy to feed to dairy cows, huge water consumption, antibiotic resistance – I could go on but you get the idea.

Nadiya is on the Case

The time has never been better for a food revolution. It's now absurdly easy to to find a recipe for just about anything online (or as my hip friends assure me, on Tiktok) replete with a sparky youngster giving a demonstration in a snappily edited video. There is a vegan copycat recipe for most of the dishes I've ever heard of and surplus besides. If you google 'vegan recipes' you get 3,340,000,000 hits. Truth be told, I don't even know what that number is but it's undeniably a lot of choice and certainly easier than when you had to wait for someone in your family to die so you inherited a copy of *Mrs Beeton*. Although, fair warning, some are written by Yanks who therefore feel compelled to describe everything as 'flavorful' and 'addicting' which shits me no end, but Rome wasn't built in a day.

The Obesity Analogy

We live in an obesogenic society. That means that it's borderline impossible to eat, exercise and exist in a way that is apart from and independent of the absolutely batshit food culture we have created. People living with obesity are not lazy, greedy Fatty Fatsons, but rather a member or a species living in an environment to which we are not biologically or psychologically suited. People cannot avoid eating the products of the food environment in which we exist. Similarly, we live in an ecologically injurious environment. People cannot avoid damaging the planet an unreasonable amount because of the way we live in the West – because we live in a culture that is set up to be extractive and destructive. There are, of course, exceptions – the extreme and the extremely wealthy. Shit loads of cash enables you to sustain yourself on wheatgrass shots, bullet coffees shat out by some magical Nicaraguan limas and raw kale salads. Loads of cash enables you to hire a nutritionist, a chef, a personal trainer and plan your days around healthy meal times and habits and get 8 hours of sleep a night after scrolling through the shiny people on Instagram. Loads of cash lets you buy solar panels for your house, drive a fancy Tesla, eschew supermarket beef for locally reared, organic topside, carbon offset your seventh flight of the year and sneer at and judge those people popping through the Macdonald's Drive-Thru after their 10 hour shift because they're too damn tired to cook a vegetable lasagne that no-one wants to eat.

Admission time: I'm a social climber and I'm good at it. I'm also part of a transitional generation. Both of my grandmothers lived in social housing. Both of my parents left school at 16. Neither went to university. I am, however, very obviously middle class with no real concept of the struggles I've avoided by a temporal whisker. I have never known hunger, want or deprivation but I'm in close enough generational proximity to it to recognise that the green movement has a problem. A class one. We are in very real danger of having green matters being dismissed as a rich, white people issue. Sure, there are plenty of rich, white, prolix hippie twats who wave the eco banner around, at volume, but there is a major issue created by people reassuring themselves that eco-activism is a bougie fad...

If society already treats you badly, the ecological crisis will exacerbate this. Think of this as ecological intersectionality. This is like paying unaffordable rent to live on the corner of Shafted Avenue and Screwed Over Drive. It sucks. Twice. As Jonathon Porritt says, 'with a broken planet, we will have no gay rights, no feminism, no respect for trans people, no attempt at fairness and justice for people of colour.' Structural racism, sexism, ableism and all of the other ugly 'isms' we subject each other to are going to be made so much worse by the impacts of climate change. Just as the pandemic highlighted the worn crotch of society's trousers, the growing ecological breakdown will expose every waistband that's too tight, every jacket that no longer keeps out the rain and every social security net that has revealed itself to be full of holes.

What You Can Actually Chuffing Do:

1. Argue with your loved ones. Firstly, a heated argument probably means you can crank the thermostat down a bit and secondly, having a little chat with people you care about regarding why they need to care about the planet and take their bags for life up the shops, might just do some good.

2. Take your bags for life up the shops.

3. Don't buy more stuff to be eco-friendly; my 23-year-old Sigg bottle does the same job as one of those poncey pastel jobbies. (No one likes a bottle wanker.)

4. Try to eat seasonably – we shouldn't be eating strawberries in November. Deal with it. Very helpful infographic here.[1]

5. Try to eat more locally – green beans air-freighted from Kenya are not going to help this crisis.

6. Batch cook – large batches use relatively less packaging and energy to cook. Give any leftovers to friends and neighbours so they say nice things about you when you die.

7. Before you die, make your desire for an eco-friendly cardboard coffin known.

8. Flush your toilet less often. Little bit of a pee pond never hurt anyone.

---

[1] https://eatseasonably.co.uk

9. If you must breed, breastfeed if you can.

10. Buy. Less. Shit.

Chapter 5
Must Do Better

So, how long have you been a dick/vegan for now, Emma?

I have to level with you (and possibly should not have waited until Chapter 5 to do so).

I am not vegan. Not yet anyway. Before you start muttering about what a filthy, great hypocrite I am, hear me out. There is no real excuse for me not having ditched the animal products. None whatsoever. I know that by eating them I'm both breaking the planet more than necessary and being complicit in some pretty shady animal welfare ethics (*cheep cheep*).

Well, it sure as hell sounds like you're working up to an excuse Emma...

I'm genuinely not. I have none. *Mea culpa* – again. I had my cousin and his wife over for lunch yesterday and we had pizza (cheese) and melting chocolate puddings (butter, eggs, chocolate). Lots of people genuinely don't know how bad our environmental crisis is – some even through no fault of their own (although there are plenty of people being ostrich dicks too). However, I'm not one of them. I *know*, thanks to reading 30 plus books (*alright, specky four eyes*) on the subject, all written by people who practise what they preach…So why can't I put my big girl pants on and stop being a dick? This is a really uncomfortable question, and it seems like lots of the wonderful environmental activists are all out there living their best, shiny vegan lives and not being bloody great hypocrites like me. Apart from a nice man called Jonathan Safran Foer. He too *knows* and yet has flirted with steak and chicken wings for much of his adult life and still isn't quite able to commit to being a full-time dick/vegan. So, what is it that's so hard about taking the plunge into what Jonathan and I *know* is morally right? This isn't me being a sanctimonious dick. I think it's a fairly straightforward moral argument to say that continuing to eat a diet that is hurting the environment and will cause increasing levels of suffering to other members of humanity is ethically shady as fuck. What's worse is, I am still not vegan because I *enjoy* animal products. So, me putting nice things in my mouth matters more than people's physical welfare – wow, and you thought I was being a dick about the vegan at Christmas thing.

This is where this whole thing gets distasteful on a personal level. We can all readily be appalled by little asylum-seeking children being washed up, drowned on Greek beaches, can wring our hands about the Californian wildfires, weep over the skinny, malnourished polar bears that get smoked by a walrus tusk wound – and yet the white chocolate I'm eating while I'm typing tastes so nice. I wish that was a fake illustration but I'm genuinely eating white chocolate while I type this. It's not even FairTrade. Authoring a book on the climate emergency affords an opportunity for me to pledge (virtue signal) to cease my consumption of animal products on publication or some such *#vowtobevegan* bullshit. But the fact that even whiny, "I really want to save the planet," me, can't walk away from the fondant fancies, illustrates what a massive shift our food culture will have to make.

Hypocritical Oath

Mark Boyle wrote that, 'hypocrisy might be the highest ideal of all.' Evidently, vegans have been getting it all wrong and whilst no one is losing any sleep if vegans are unpopular, this is problematic because people also don't like the message they're spelling out with pulled jackfruit. We have, of course, seen all this before. Who else didn't people like? The Puritans. They lectured all their mates about what horrible people they were and how they were never going to get into heaven if they insisted upon nice church decor and anything that smelled even faintly Catholic. They wanged on about it so much, it was better for them to cross the Atlantic Ocean for a fresh start rather than sit in foment across the table from all the people they'd upset. Granted, the ecumenical disputes were a shade more complex than this but I'm not a bloody historian. Short version: the Puritans held very different views from the status quo and so it was better that they left (on a long and dangerous sea voyage rather than continue to rub people up the wrong way) to start a new life in Massachusetts where they could do as much no laughing, no talking as they liked.

Life is not clean eating, sleep hygiene and eight glasses of filtered water a day. Life is messy. Life is family arguments, being annoyed with your mates and being short-tempered with your spouse for their inability to stack the dishwasher correctly. (Honestly, I'm the bane of my husband's existence.) What about if we offered veganism in a new incarnation to people? Say, buttered toast for breakfast and chickpea salad for tea…Perhaps, not all of us can reasonably be expected to 100% vegan, 100% of the time. Also, it puts people off – trying to commit to perfection sounds terribly dull and completely unattainable. Veganism needs to be much more of a dip your toe in, drop-in centre type food culture rather than some shiny, perfection-toting lifestyle choice. This is possibly where the term 'plant-based' is more appropriate because, although it sounds pretty wanky, it seems to afford slightly more fallibility than your average bhaji burger. Vegan is perceived as a bit too close to wagon and it's a big step up and a long fall down from that apparatus.

Maybe my friend who saves tuckered out bumble bees but gladly eats lamb is right; you cannot adopt a lofty position of perfection perched atop pillars of quinoa. Maybe you can do some things right and that's enough. Minimal gains. Less white chocolate, fewer pizzas.

Hang on Emma, you sound a little conflicted – I thought we all had to go vegan?

Don't we all pal, don't we all?

What Can/Should We Do?

Whilst diligent recycling (so we can ship it to Asia where it's burnt, poisoning the locals and emitting more toxins into the atmosphere), switching to an electric vehicle (making you complicit in the ethically dubious lithium mining industry) and signing Greenpeace petitions on Facebook (*dusts off hands* – that's me sorted for eco activism for the next fortnight) are laudable and all that, compared to tackling the emissions caused by animal agriculture, they are worth sweet. fuck. all. Nobody wants to stand up in front of an army/country/gathering of extended family and tell them that they can never eat the nice things again. No-one. Not even me – and I really like the sound of my own voice and have been known to be a touch belligerent. People are going to be upset, going to rebel and it will inevitably get ugly. There is going to be a huge shift in our local and global food culture or we are all going to fucking die from starvation/climate change/war.

Unfortunately for the sausage baps, 'the biggest difference we can make as individuals – and, collectively, to the carbon footprint of food – is to eat less meat.' Chris Goodall really knows how to kill a buzz/bap.

But sausage baps with brown sauce are so tasty...

It pains me to tell you this but all roads where we survive as a species, lead to Dick/Vegan Town. I'll let that sink in a bit. We are all going to turn into dicks. Well, not every last one of us. Rich twats will still totally live by their own set of rules because: money. But for most people, you included, your life will feature fewer animal products as the next half century plays out. It would also flatter my ego tremendously if you cut a few animal products from your diet after reading this and I promise not to let it go to my head.

Something very interesting came out of Covid in terms of vegetables – every Tom, Dick and wanker decided they wanted to live *The Good Life* (well, all the wealthy people with outdoor space anyway) and dig a vegetable patch in their gardens. People responded to the crisis by trying to improve their own food security by rolling their sleeves up and grabbing a spade. People did not start trying to buy cows or sheep on eBay – it was vegetable staples that were accessible and unless the gardeners were total fuckwits, plentiful. (I'll be open: I ballsed up courgettes last summer – yes, *courgettes*, for heaven's sake.)

Yeah, but ploughing is causing soil erosion (you said so yourself) and so if we all stop eating beef and start eating tofu, we're still screwing the planet as the soybeans are still being sown, grown and irrigated, you dick.

Well, yes but, in a future vegan food culture, we're not growing more soy beans than humans eat to feed to cows who also drink a metric fuck tonne of water, are dosed with antibiotics prophylactically to promote faster growth and fart their nasty methane guffs which is doing a right job on our knackered atmosphere. (Who feels like a dick now?) It is imperative we reduce the number of livestock on Earth – there really isn't any getting away from this.

But Being a Vegan Will Be Horrible, Won't It?

Yes and no. Being a vegan means no late night doner kebabs, no crispy fried chicken, no bacon butties, no lamb bhunas, no fillet steak, no 30p hotdogs at Scandanavian furniture shops – the meals we know, love and mark our lives with will have to go. They will change and evolve. Or we all destroy life on Earth. And, just to be clear, if we fuck the planet over royally because we wanted to hang onto Big Macs by our fingernails (other industrially farmed, mass-produced burgers are available), there won't be any Big Macs either because it's kind of hard to get to the drive-thru if there's a civil war caused by resource scarcity going on – FYI.

Potentially, we may need to aggressively re-brand veganism because, even though I wrote a book about how the vegans were right, every time I see the word I still mutter "dicks" under my breath. Perhaps we could have a whip-round and pay the people who had the unenviable task of promoting this book to have a crack (kind of a tough sell given that I am not a well-known DJ writing a children's book. Not that they'd let me write a children's book – too much fucking swearing). In an attempt to improve vegan PR, I have compiled a (potentially inaccurate) list of people I think are cool who are also vegan. At the time of writing, none of these people had been implicated in sexual misconduct/going to Barnard Castle, but you know how it is these days.

Beyonce – like I even need to explain.

Venus Williams – tennis legend.

Sam Ryder – he persuaded Europeans to hate us less and sings like an angel.

Elliot Page – boss actor.

Liam Hemsworth – mostly why I was motivated to marry an Australian.

Peter Dinklage – actor who carried Game of Thrones. I know I'm right on this.

Joaquin Pheonix – a lot of actors are but he seems like a nice human too.

Stevie Wonder – course he is, bloody legend.

Lewis Hamilton – quite good at driving.

Alan Cummings – best Bond baddie ever.

Colin Kaepernick – incredible football player, incredibler human.

Back to us all agreeing that we're going to go vegan. So, it's not likely to prove easy but here are some reasons to remind you why it's important. A bunch of annoying, clever dicks at the University of Oxford have said that going vegan is the 'single biggest way' to reduce how much you fuck the planet up. I'm paraphrasing, but you get the gist. Ok, given this is important, what Joseph Poore actually said was, 'A vegan diet is probably the single biggest way to reduce your impact on planet Earth, not just greenhouse gases, but global acidification, eutrophication, land use and water use…It is far bigger than cutting down on your flights or buying an electric car.' Firstly, and pleasingly, his assertion gets me off the hook for driving round my big, dirty, diesel van (win!) but he really does seem pretty confident that we need to step away from the industrially farmed animal products.

There is a caveat with the whole vegans will change the future schtick…they won't. Whilst we absolutely do need to stop hoeing through the meat, milk and eggs, we also need to ensure people are informed about why they can't have a bacon buttie. The oil companies have rather a lot to answer for – because they have long known climate change is a direct result of burning fossil fuels and because they paid for a lot of spurious scientific studies that enabled them to deny it – for a really long time. Where I'm from we call this lying and then paying millions of dollars to hide your lies. Of course, they are only acting in their own best interests, but they must be a thing of the past.

If green energy is such a good idea, why aren't they all getting into the renewables market with gusto?

Unfortunately, once a wind turbine is erected (snicker) it has an irritating ability to generate virtually limitless and virtually free energy. If people have lots of free energy, the commodity is no longer of much value. And oil companies operate on the premise of having the whole world by the short and curlies – they have something valuable that we want, and we give them lots of cash in order to get our grubby hands on it. Not only do we need to stop the profligate use of fossil fuels in agriculture – fertilisers, transportation, farm machinery – we also need to leave fossil fuels in the ground/under the sea/in the well so certain Texans don't get mega rich and end up in public office.

There is a final reminder regarding what we need to do next.

Lots and lots fewer animal products.

No fossil fuels.

Oh, and, crucially,

DON'T VOTE FOR DICKS!

But What the Fuck Am I Meant to Eat?

It should be noted that some of the plant-based products are getting seriously good. Last Sunday's Family Tea Time (my husband and I can only stomach eating with the kids once a week because they want their tea at fucking 4pm which means I'm drunk and hungry again by 7) featured burgers so bloody good, I swear they were nicer than a beef burger and I got to feel all smug about my eco credentials in eating it. We had the *Beyond Burger* with mustard, ketchup, lettuce, tomato, gherkins (not my husband, he's a philistine) and even though I'm not being paid by them for an endorsement, they were delicious and I can't really see why you *would* eat a beef burger. (I definitely *should* be being paid for this endorsement.) Plus, there is one more cow out there, still licking its own nostrils and blinking its unfeasibly long eyelashes.

Far be it for me to claim to be a culinary whizz but I can cook a bit (entirely thanks to my mum, and her mum before her, and her mum who was in service). Something that does seem rather daunting to lots of plant-based-curious people is: what the fuck are you meant to feed the family? A legitimate question. Big overshare here but here's a little peek at a week's worth of meals that my household tolerates. Please note that my children are on a different menu because you know children and how flexible they are with their dietary habits.

- **Monday:** Refried beans, rice and lettuce tacos
- **Tuesday:** Satay vegetable stir fry with noodles and peanuts
- **Wednesday:** Burritos with black beans
- **Thursday:** Freezer meal of oven chips and bean burgers with coleslaw and gherkins
- **Friday:** Cauliflower jalfrezi, pilau rice and rotis
- **Saturday:** Pizza night. Bought some vegan cheese off Facebook (possibly the worst fucking place to buy cheese, ever)
- **Sunday:** Green Thai vegetable curry soup (still hunting for a vegan green Thai curry paste)

Fuck me, just realised how much rice we eat. And if memory serves me, I'm pretty sure rice isn't great for the planet. Flooded paddy fields release a lot of methane which is worse than…shit. I probably should have dressed it up a bit more so I looked more eco-conscious but, as I think you've guessed by now, whilst I do have a bit of a thing for saving the planet but I'm not claiming to be Mary fucking Poppins.

Doing a Jamie

In 2005 the TV series *Jamie's School Dinners* aired in the UK, and it enabled the middle classes to laugh and scoff at poor people and their terrible diets while they smugly watched their own kids snack on crudités and pots of organic hummus. Cynics felt it was another headline-grabbing programme, devised to create a stir. I happen to disagree and believe that Jamie Oliver truly cares about food education and healthy nutrition for ordinary people. Moreover, that this agenda he pushes is not a money-making opportunity but something he's passionate about – not least because he doesn't seem to be very good at making money as most of his businesses went bust in 2019 so try not to be so insensitive. The food inequalities in Great Britain in the 2020s are still vast and pernicious. People don't get to choose where they live, the circumstances they endure or the hand they are dealt. Many politicians cannot get their tiny minds around this which is why they said such ignorant, mean-spirited things about the recipients of free school meals – the absence of which was hugely traumatic for the hungry children in question during the lockdowns. Just a reminder, 320 Conservative MPs voted against free school meals over the holidays to try to mitigate the deprivation made more acute by the effects of the pandemic. In exemplary humanitarian fashion, one MP used it as an opportunity to spaff moralistic nonsense about how we should, instead be, 'encouraging absent parents to take some responsibility for their children.' Hell, somewhere, a Dickens novel is missing its villain. As many people pointed out, it was just a touch embarrassing that they could find the cash to subsidise the Eat Out, to Help Out scheme (which turned out to be a major driver of covid infections in Wave 57 of The Plague Without End) but were too skint to help hungry children.

Emma, I think Nigel Farage famously tweeted something along the lines of this…are you a closet Make Britain a First Rate Coloniser Again, loon?

I shan't dignify that with a response but I will say that when everyone murmurs, "he *does* have a point," about one of the most hated politicians in the country, it does beg the question whether the leadership team are sociopaths.

Why Don't People Like Vegans?

There are many reasons why vegans get a bad rap. Lots of people's subconscious helpfully conjures up a sanctimonious and garrulous wanker that wants to smugly tell you what a bad person you are. None of us like being made to feel like an arsehole (although many of us bloody love pointing judgy fingers at others) and veganism is a heady mixture of feeling bad about being mean to animals and the planet. Vegans are mostly made, not born – most people aren't raised vegan. They find veganism or convert to it, and you know that old truism about converts and zeal – it makes people come across as kind of a dick.

Now, if you cast your mind back to the beginning of the book where I writ my small-minded personality flaws good and large, I spoke of my knee jerk reaction for having to cater for someone who ate differently to me. In *my* home, at *my* table, at *Christmas*. Even I wouldn't have been so snotty about cooking different food if someone was coeliac (although I totally would if they 'avoided gluten' because none of us have time for that snake oil) or had another medical reason for their differing requirements. Sharing a meal is ancient and culturally important, typically because you share the same food and therefore enjoy a common experience. Unless the cooking is awful – then you share horrid food and potentially the bathroom a couple of hours later. This shared experience is less shared and somewhat more awkward if one person is munching on a mushroom wellington while everyone else devours a steak. It creates a distance at an event that's supposed to be about closeness and conviviality. Moreover, unlike the blessèd Cranks era vegetarians, who politely ate around the meat components of the meal or picked at the side dishes without making a fuss, vegans require a whole different approach to cooking. Most meals/food items need several components substituting/altering. Also, vegans have a tendency to be a teeny bit more vocal than your garden variety vegetarian and share their reasons for making this particular dietary choice. Perhaps we all need to accept that just keeping schtum and not mentioning poor animal welfare and how we're breaking the ecosystem isn't doing any of us any favours. Maybe this is the Me Too moment for ecology? Maybe we need to stop having a society-wide code of silence and instead speak out about the very real consequences of our diets. *#mootoo?*

White Sauce

Good God woman, isn't it enough that you're another educated, white woman who's got a book published?

Relax – I'm going to get all homespun on you now.

One of my first memories of cooking is when my mum (the one who doesn't like swearing, awkward) taught me to make white sauce for a dish she calls cauliflower supper – it's basically cauliflower cheese but with whatever is lurking at the bottom of the fridge thrown in for good measure/to clear out the bottom of the fridge.

Incidentally, you can do a better job than the national census of gauging people's class by asking them whether they consider cauliflower cheese a side dish (dreadfully posh, pass me the *Debrett's*) or a main meal (do use the couch for your feet, pet). Suffice to say, it's a main meal in my house. Recently my mum and her four siblings got together for dinner and they had cauliflower cheese – for dinner – at a get together. I ribbed her for this before she reminded me that growing up in a single parent family with six mouths to feed meant that food was not something to be taken for granted and that I was being a knob. So far, so normal. I was lucky to have a parent who both knew how to cook and had the time and desire to teach me those skills. I think almost anyone can learn how to cook but it is a skill that has to be learnt – and therefore taught in some fashion. Presently, it's very easy to watch cooking programmes and find recipes on the internet but food cultures are phenomenally localised. I can cook, my brother would admit that he cannot. Granted, he's not going to starve (finally, the patriarchy is useful) but cookery knowledge is the alchemy between necessity, interest and opportunity. I have been lucky to have all three. Real world healthy cooking needs to be taught in schools to ensure that people who don't come from rich food cultures, are equipped with the skills to feed themselves affordably and healthily. Ideally, they'd be able to afford some ingredients too. Levelling Up and all that.

A Nation of Dog-Owning Shopkeepers

We like animals. We also like eating animals. This is a well known and passionately debated psychological phenomenon called the meat paradox or selective carnivorism, which I mentioned earlier. In brief, it's the idea that we stroke cats but chow on catfish, we sponsor dolphins but eat bratwurst, we have our dogs at our weddings but teach hundreds of people how to snare and gut rabbits before brushing them with honey and thyme and barbecuing over the coals.

You had your dog at your wedding? Weirdo.

I'm happy to have a lot of my personality assassinated (it's a legitimate target) and do a bit of teacher bashing (sorry Hubs) and farmer moralising (it's coming, fear not) but I will *not* have people speak ill of my dog. Tally is my beloved 10-year-old black Labrador and she is the core of my family. I'm utterly and hopelessly besotted with her. She *gets* me, is a fabulous walking companion and is probably the reason I didn't totally lose my mind to Postpartum Anxiety after the birth of my first child. She is very much not 'just a dog.' I recognise her sentience and her intelligence as at least on a par with (the former) if not exceeding (the latter) my own.

Christ, you're weird about trees and *animals. Fantastic.*

Actually, I'm weird about trees and dogs – not animals in general. Frankly, I can take or leave cats, horses, gerbils, iguanas and chinchillas. But dogs. Love them, love, love, love them. So yes, I had my dog at my wedding because although there were only 16 humans there (including the Priest, me and my betrothed) she warranted an invitation. I love her that much. I love her so much that a couple of hours after getting hitched I sat down to eat some other animals that weren't dogs. Because only a psycho would eat dogs. And therein lies the paradox – eating some animals is wrong and weird, eating other animals is right and totally normal. Reflecting on the arbitrary nature of these assignations makes your head spin a bit/feel bad for eating chicken wings. Some of these awkward ruminations are good to sit with for a while. Make yourself feel uncomfortable in order to motivate yourself to reduce your reliance on animal products – it's a much better use of time than 98% of what we do on our phones.

Oh yeah, that Kae Tempest song about looking at our phones instead of watching Earth die.

That's the one. Happy days.

Who Maimed Roger Rabbit?

As I mentioned, during the course of my work as an outdoors education instructor, one of the skills I taught was how to catch a rabbit (*Oryctolagus cuniculus*), kill it, skin, butcher and cook it. My colleagues and I would share knowing smiles about the people who were committed carnivores until they had had a direct hand in preparing from point of kill, that night's tea. Some commercially available rabbit meat is farmed, much is 'lamped' (involving night time excursions with a bright light and a rifle) and some is snared. As a rule, I genuinely consider game (venison, rabbit, wild fowl) to be some of the most humane meat available. I think in large part because if I had to choose between a happy outdoors life running about the place before I got shot while I was trying to figure out what that light was or being born in a crate, taken from my mother before weaning and injected with medicines to mitigate the conditions that economics forced me to be kept in, I'd choose the former.

One slightly less touchy feely way of catching a rabbit is snaring. Something I now feel crummy about is that I taught a lot of people (oh ok, 99% of whom were men) how to manufacture a snare. I also taught them how to dispatch a rabbit that they had been lucky enough to catch in said snare. You need to come up to it from behind – I'd like to say to limit its distress but really it's so that you don't get scratched to buggery. A rabbit is a muscular animal and they will fight fiercely as they cannily sense you might be thinking about eating them. Using one hand to pin it by the back of the neck and the other to grab its back legs, you lift the rabbit up and (I'm a righty) grasping it by the back legs with your left hand as if you're holding a bunch of flowers, use your right hand to make your first two fingers into bunny ears (an unfortunate irony) you place a finger either side of its neck and roll your knuckle into its spine, simultaneously lifting its chin and stretching the rabbit so as to separate its spinal column. If you do it well, this only takes a couple of seconds and despite some twitching, its neck will be floppy and it is dead and insensible.

Sensible consumers check under the hood for any problems. When butchering, you can check the health of the rabbit (well, what its health was like – it's clearly not great by this point) by looking at its organs to look for signs of disease or illness. Livers tell no lies and rabbits in the early stage of Myxomatosis might look ok with their jackets on but their livers tell a different, lesion-covered story. You can eat a mixy rabbit – this is a bunny that is infected with Myxomatosis – a viral disease that was introduced to reduce the number of wild rabbits in the UK because we'd killed all the predators and this caused a glitch in the ecosystem.

Hang on, we used biological weapons, in our own country, on rabbits?

As I was saying, you can eat a rabbit that has been infected with Myxomatosis but given how well things are going with zoonotic diseases of late, I wouldn't.

This was a demonstration I gave many, many times before going on to show my students how to skin, butcher and cook a rabbit. As the lecture progressed, I would often find my students becoming increasingly subdued and sombre. All of a sudden, smashing a whole bucket of chicken after a night on the lash didn't seem like quite such good fun. Most of us could no sooner walk through an abattoir followed by 'the works' at a steakhouse than we could butcher and barbeque the family dog. Most of us are (mercifully) disconnected to the realities of meat production. It's perhaps no coincidence that we really started to screw the planet up around the same time we figured out how to mass produce meat. It's both a discrete and a related pair of issues. We eat too much meat thus damaging the planet and we are able to eat so much meat because we have developed fiendishly efficient but inhumane systems for rearing animals which are so inhumane, most of us don't have the stomach to understand too intimately. As George Monbiot says, 'we don't want to consider the scale of the suffering our diet demands.'

Because we are ignorant (wilfully so) about how cows and pigs and sheep get from the transport truck to our plates, we are able to ignore the cost that is inherent to meat. We can look away.

Speaking of Looking Away...

Why don't people care more about the environment?

Meanwhile in Gilead, plenty of people are fighting other battles. Big and important ones. Marginalised groups are already exhausting their time and resources to pursue equal rights for LGBTQA+ people, for people of colour, for food for hungry children. A reminder that in Afghanistan, women are back to arguing for the right to have a visible face (in addition to the right to an education) which you'd think wouldn't be the tallest order but never underestimate the crazy of a group of dudes interpreting a religious text to suit their own ends. Whilst researching this book, I was reading another book called *Timeless Simplicity* whilst juggling open documents, my phone and precariously balancing my laptop on my baby. It's ok – she was asleep – or at least she was until I dropped my phone on her. Our world is complicated AF. We messed up. I like to blame my current level of scatty on Long Covid but I suspect it's got more to do with the modern world; it's completely bonkers. We live at a ridiculously frenetic pace and, don't interrupt me, I'm over caffeinated, but this doesn't leave much free time for 'good works' and in which to research burgeoning social justice issues. What we need for everyone to understand is that if the environment collapses, everything else will all go to shit too. Good environmental health facilitates all of the other societal goods that we need to champion – otherwise they will be shuffled down the global to-do list at a rate of knots.

We Need to Talk About Farmers

So, this is going to hurt – and a great deal more than a former doctor whinging about women wanting bodily autonomy as a human exits their nethers. Farming needs to be revolutionised. Fast. Farmers are good people (for the most part, although some are, of course, dickheads) trying to do the spectacularly difficult job of feeding us while the climate gets increasingly unpredictable, they get screwed over by the major retailers and everyone has a go at them. This is perhaps one of the reasons it's an ageing workforce. In 2016, 84% of farm holders were male, 40% of those were over 65 years old and the median age was 60. Farmers are also overwhelmingly white – which some people say benignly reflects the lower levels of diversity in rural communities but one might be so bold as to suggest that the industry isn't managing to attract a more representative cross section of society. This isn't me lining up to take pot shots at beleaguered farmers – I swear but, much like other areas of society, a workforce should reflect the people it serves.

The first thing we all forget to do is to say thank you to the hardworking hands that feed us.

Given what hard graft farming is, people aren't working beyond retirement age for shits and giggles. I would hazard that many of them can't afford to retire after working for low wages for their entire lives, many are in tied accommodation which means they're out of a house as soon as they stop working and for those with farms to pass on, their own offspring may well be displaying a reluctance to enter an industry that treats people thus.

So, farmers, thank you.

Really, I mean it.

Don't Bite the Hand That Feeds You

"If you knew what your best friend said about you behind your back, you'd kill yourself."

So, this is the hill you've chosen to die on? Making light of suicide?

Actually, no. Bear with me. This was something a university lecturer (a cool one, not a creepy one) told me, and I maintain that he was spot on. Slagging off your mates is one thing but slagging off the people who put food in your bellies is like slagging off your mate when she's taken you out for dinner and she's paying – rude *and* inadvisable. Of late, we've decided we quite like to bash a farmer in the UK (ironic, really, given we also like to bash a vegan). It has become fashionable to criticise them for the cruelty and effects of the farming system they operate within. Farmers have little to no choice but to adhere to the 'rules' as written by the major retailers if they don't want to get into huge debt. The stress of the decisions that farmers have to make shouldn't be underestimated. Nor should Big Agriculture be confused with the people who toil to feed us 365 days a year.

Farmers' Anonymous

Once we dramatically reduce the numbers of livestock we rear and consume, there are going to be rather a lot of unhappy and unoccupied livestock farmers. Moreover, what will the middle classes do with their offspring on weekends and half terms if they can't go to the local Farm Park? You can't expect the kiddies to get excited about looking at the turnips or watering the sugar beets. Although it's certainly one way of addressing the Brexit-aggravated farm labour shortage – minors don't qualify for minimum wage either – bonus.

We need some sort of Special Advisor to Farmers that somehow, miraculously bucks the systemic and endemic issue of such post-holders being astoundingly unqualified for their posts. Much as (unqualified) government ministers or indeed the then Lord Chancellor might claim that people 'have had enough of experts,' I contrarily believe that it is of the utmost importance that we involve farming experts on this one. And a 'farming expert' must have at least successfully worked on a farm – as a baseline. Imagine how much less chaos would have ensued in the education sector had Gove, as I noted earlier, actually worked in a school and therefore had the tiniest inkling of what it's like at the coalface. His Levelling Up position went swimmingly too. It should also be a pre-requisite that, even if they left school at 16 to run their family farm, if they've been busted watching porn at work, they don't make the shortlist.

Five for Farming

Farming needs a bit of TLC. Like most people who don't work in marketing (and many of those who do) I assume that the best way to sell something is to make it sexy. I'm not suggesting that we make farming sexy in the fashion of those rather passé topless farmhand calendars/Jilly Cooper book covers (nor would that serve to address the gender imbalance in farming), but sexy enough that it becomes an appealing industry to work in. Having a shortage of farm workers and future managers is somewhat like having a shortage of air to breathe – we're going to come a cropper pretty quickly and spectacularly. We could achieve this by a simple two step process:

Step 1 – Stop bashing farmers as being the root of all environmental evil (aviation industry, I'm coming for you) and try to be grateful for them keeping all of us alive. May I remind you that if you like eating, you like farmers. We really, really can't 'cancel' farmers.

Step 2 – Devise a huge programme to train, recruit and retain ecologically friendly, sustainable and regenerative farming sorts and while we're on my wish list, a cohort that accurately represents the diversity of gender, ethnicity and sexual orientation of our population.

Nice idea but you're sounding a bit sketchy on some of the details.

Hey, I'm the engineer, not the oily rag and my spoons aren't going to whittle themselves.

So, after we've made farming into an industry that no longer feels like you'd have to be deranged to want to enter, we need to overhaul what we farm and what we eat.

How original. Banging the vegan drum again, Emma?

You *did* read the title of the book, right?

Give Me Spots on My Apples

Back in 1962 we received an important memo from an eminent environmentalist, warning us that we risked a silent spring (because all the nature was dead). She cleverly titled the book *Silent Spring* just so that people could be sure what she was talking about, and so that the agrochemical companies knew who to direct their lawsuits at. Rachel Carson warned us about this mess 60 years ago. My mum was 4 at the time – she is now a grandmother but we are *still* not taking care of our environment. Artists got on board and Joni Mitchell reminded us in 1970 that DDT was not a clever solution to a pest problem, but rather a poison that persists for a long time in the environment. This particular tonic is now only licenced for use against malarial mosquitoes, but we still really like spaffing unpleasant things all over our green and pleasant land.

The two major shifts needed in agriculture to save the planet are dramatically reducing the number of livestock we rear and moving to as close to organic farming as possible. Guy Singh-Watson has warned this may be 'a painful process; depending on the level of degradation, it takes up to five years for soils to recover and adjust to life without nitrogen fertiliser.' He added, 'Converting the mindset of a farmer raised on agrochemicals can take even longer.' Like many of the mitigations to the climate emergency, the brilliant ideas we implement will take time to bear fruit and so we need to implement them yesterday. Time really is of the essence (for future human existence, no biggie).

Agrochemical manufacturing is big business and is worth over £1 billion per annum in the UK alone. Some of the products a typical company supplies farms with are herbicides, fungicides, insecticides, 'crop nutrition' (fertiliser), adjuvants and conditioners (literally no clue what these do), biostimulants and bafflingly 'Irish Products.' The best bit is the names. You can spaff delights such as Glow, Fathom, Promise or, my personal favourite Explicit all over your crops. Actually, maybe I'm late to the party – it sounds as though someone is already trying to make farming sexy. Although reading that – they're clearly not going about it in the right way. I need to get my miniature violin out again – the agrochemical companies cannot and will not be able to operate as they currently do. Mining for phosphates, using fossil fuel origin fertilisers and trying to apply chemical sticking plasters to the soil that we continue to degrade is not sustainable – it's going to stop working. If it stops working, we stop eating and may arrive in what some scientists are calling the post agricultural epoch. This isn't an era when we can create food using magic. It's an era when we're going to starve. Here's the rub – it's farming that has given us nice lives – really nice lives. With leisure time and Netflix and public sewerage and universal healthcare. If your consultant is too busy foraging for berries, she won't have time to do your knee replacement. Agricultural systems facilitate pretty much everything you can think of. Subsistence living is really hard work – not to mention completely laughable at our current population density. (Yes, my bad, *again*.) We need agriculture; we just need to make it better. Agrochemical companies are good at teaming up with Big Agriculture to lobby so as to ensure maximum profits. We need to get wise to these tactics/ban the shit out of them.

I'm a Survivor

You can survive for about three weeks without food, three days without water and about three minutes without air. (And somewhere between one and five minutes without checking your phone when you're meant to be writing a book.) If the farmers went on a two-week strike, people would die. If nothing else, we ought to be nicer to them from a point of self-interest. I, more than most Westerners, know exactly how much hard work and precarity goes into living a subsistence lifestyle – a pre-agrarian, living from the land existence. It's entirely ridiculous to suppose that we have enough great reedmace (*Typha latifolia*) or chicken of the woods (*Laetiporus sulphureus*) to feed more than a handful of us. Plus, most people aren't able to identify much beyond a daffodil (*Narcissus*) because we don't teach children anything important about the natural world, and they would probably poison themselves. The former looks a lot like irises and often grow side by side and the latter is a fungus and, you know fungi: you can eat *all* of them but, some of them, only once. Agriculture is what has given us the gift of civilisation – sanitation, healthcare systems, the opportunity of universal education – even if we prefer giving this more consistently to boys. We need to heal our agricultural system and remove power from the huge conglomerates that include the agrochemical giants, Big Chicken, Big Dairy and start calling out money for the pernicious influence it wields.

Agroecology

Despite appearances, this isn't an irate ecologist, nor is it some new-fangled approach to farming that means we all have to share three sunflower seeds between us a week. It's a system of farming that is sustainable and means we will be able to have food to eat next year as well as this one, that our children and grandchildren will also have food to eat. Overhauling our food system and diets is going to cause a lot of change in a short space of time. In terms of weaning ourselves off of chemical fertilisers and pesticides, this is going to directly translate to smaller yields, less reliable harvests and potentially quite serious crop failures and food stuffs shortage – although these risks aren't as large as the agrochemical industry would have you believe. Much like the gun lobby, creating a culture of fear where people feel compelled to buy more and more guns/pesticides so that we can reliably have mass shootings/poison our pollinators and water courses, is good for business. Dramatically reducing our consumption of meat and animal products is an essential part of the necessary changes to our food culture which will mean our menus need to be changed pretty dramatically, pretty quickly.

The alternative though is worse – if we continue to eke out the highest yield harvests from knackered soils, there won't be any land that is much cop for farming left nor any pollinators to pollinate the things we need to eat.

What You Can Actually Chuffing Do:

I can't very well wang on about sodding cauliflower cheese and then not tell you how to make a really good vegan version.

Cauliflower Cheese/Supper Recipe
1 cauliflower
2 tbsp rapeseed oil
1 pint alternative milk – I use oat
2 tbsp cornflour
4 tbsp nutritional yeast/nooch
1 tsp Dijon mustard
Handful of breadcrumbs

Break down cauliflower into chunks and microwave or steam until tender. Drain and set aside in an ovenproof dish. Pop oil into a pan and warm, add cornflour and stir with whisk on a low heat to cook out. Add the milk slowly, whisking constantly. When combined, slowly bring to a simmer whilst the sauce thickens. Season and add the mustard and nooch. Pour sauce over the cauliflower and sprinkle with the breadcrumbs and a good pinch of sea salt. Bake for about 20 minutes at 180 degrees.

Serve with thick slices of white bread slathered with margarine and plenty of black pepper.

Chapter 6
Dicks Galore

What, I can't have a chapter thus titled but Pussy Galore can be an actual female human's name in a *James Bond* movie?! I cry foul.

I hope that by now, thoroughly convinced by my sparkling wit and ribald cussing, you are a fully fledged eco-wanker. Newly-enthused as you are, to follow are some contributions we can all make (in addition to being vegan, of course) to try and mop up some of this mess.

Transport

We are, most of us, lazy lardy arses who drive too much and walk/bike too little. Public transport is markedly better for the environment and whilst it's less convenient for the most part, with increasing fuel prices, it might be an increasingly sensible change to make to your routine. Driving less is a great place to start as both walking and cycling emit zero grams of carbon dioxide whereas single occupancy vehicles are a right state. We should be encouraged/strong-armed into walking/cycling and using public transport more. A good way to do this is for local authorities to invest in green public transport options and to make it cheaper. Subsidising public transport is a better use of public funds than propping up the Royal Family or bailing out private banks – you know I'm right.

Lots of non-disabled people don't walk much at all. There are lots of complex factors that cause us to focus on passing our driving tests rather than reducing fossil fuel usage. Moreover, the car vs. walk choice is hugely impacted on where you live, what you need to do and how much time the greener alternative uses. I walk a lot. Approximately 1,800 miles during the last 12 calendar months.

Yeah but you probably go on lots of holidays and walk a shit tonne of miles in a week, skewing that figure.

Nope, I have only been away from home once, for 4 days, in the last 2 years – cheers covid! Also, over the last 7 years I've either been pregnant or carrying a baby in a carrier and my current walking workout means toting 13kg (yes, I know I bounce from imperial to decimal without drawing breath – my generation are measurements broken) of toddler about the place while holding two little ones' hands and my dog's lead. I should also be honest that walking would definitely be my hobby and my location and circumstances permit me to do it every day. Equally, where I live, it's not practical to walk to the shops. I live in a rural location and whilst there happens to be a major supermarket only 2 miles away, the most direct route is along a busy A road with no footpaths – not ideal with young children and that's before my hands are full of shopping bags. I think that supermarket deliveries have an opportunity to improve the green credentials of their beastly owners. If all supermarkets ran fleets of electric delivery vans and we got out of the habit of doing a 'top up' shop three times a week, we'd save money and a lot of individual car miles. I'll gloss over the fact that plenty of women and other vulnerable members of society don't feel safe walking because it's inconvenient being raped and/or murdered but I certainly don't want anyone to feel guilty about misogyny. After all, it's not like it's a hate crime.

I am also a keen cyclist and used to be fit enough to get up Mont Ventoux without rupturing something. We need to push cycling. Hard. We need to make roads an awful lot safer for cyclists than they are at present – and helpfully, an easy way to do that is to slash the number of cars they have to share the roads with. Some gentle prodding along the lines of limiting short car journeys for non-disabled people would help with this.

Windmills of My Mind

If you are in your thirties or beyond, you may find yourself inextricably drawn to listening to daytime radio shows that encourage highly opinionated people (yeah, yeah, pot: kettle) to call in and shout lots. Recently, Jeremy Vine covered the issue of wind turbines and exposed how much of a ridiculously divisive issue it is. It tickled me just how vehemently some people rage atop their soap boxes about what a "godawful eyesore" these graceful white beasts are. I would gladly go through all the logical, sensible reasons why the anti-turbine brigade should pipe down but the NIMBY dicks would have none of it and continue to splutter over their corduroy trousers and mustard sweaters. This is a time for bulldozing nonsense-spouting eejits and telling them they can get on with it or they can stop using electricity.

Wind turbines are useless! Sometimes it's too windy for them to operate and sometimes they break down – what the hell sort of system is that?!?

Sometimes the coal powered stations they replace spew carbon into the atmosphere, raising global temperatures rendering planet Earth uninhabitable and sometimes nuclear power stations do a Chernobyl before being held hostage by a gaggle of unqualified Russians conducting some denazification…just saying. Britain is relatively windy, relatively reliably. Britain's coasts are especially windy but offshore wind farms are more expensive and more complicated to build. It just makes sense to anyone who likes living with electricity to get over the squawky "but we can *see* them!" thing. As someone who has spent a good chunk of time living without electricity, I know which side my bread is buttered on. Being someone who is pleased by wild aesthetics, I am all for a natural world that doesn't show the impact of mankind's cruddy stewardship, but that really isn't the house we're living in. It's quite ridiculous for people (rich pricks) to insist that their lovely bit of skyline remains uninterrupted by wind turbines when electricity pylons, train tracks and mile after mile of asphalt bisect very nearly all of our island nation. Wind power farming is relatively cheap and quick to set up and maintain, creates work for engineers and suppliers, oh, and it provides us with free, clean energy that isn't pumping carbon out into our atmosphere which is already decidedly peaky without any additional coal mines or nuclear power stations. (The war in Ukraine is an excuse not a defence, here.)

Confessedly, sometimes I find all this death of our planet stuff a bit dreary. My solace is escaping (in my particulate-spewing van) to the mountains of Scotland (far, far away from other people) to drink in some wilderness and tranquillity (ok, ok, and some Scotch). We really do live in a beautiful place. Sure, not all of it's 'conventionally pretty' and we all have a different aesthetic groove but there is beauty everywhere. I'm obviously not going to tell you the name of my special place. Firstly, because then you'd all go there and spoil it for me by taking selfies and speaking to me. Secondly, I can't spell it because it's in Gaelic and who needs that aggro? On the drive up we break the journey at a delightful truck stop (we're not bleedin' hedge fund managers) where my kids gorge themselves on Maccer's chips and no one gets any sleep. Almost immediately after we cross the border into Scotland, and right at the point of the journey where we are all very much 'done' for the day, you begin to see hundreds upon hundreds of windmills (you try pronouncing electricity generating wind turbines aged 3). This is because Scotland makes it much easier than England to get permission to erect (titter, titter) wind turbines. This in turn is because of someone rakishly telling us he was going to cut the 'green crap.'

I don't think I'm alone in having somewhat rose-tinted memories of the seemingly benign David Cameron as Prime Minister (2010-2016). He seemed affable enough, brushed his hair regularly and managed to play down his Bullingdon Banter rather more effectively than BoJo and Rees-Smug. However, he does have rather a lot to answer for. Well, yes, er, Brexit hasn't exactly been our finest hour ("We don't talk about Brexiiiit") but I'm referring more specifically to the time in 2013 when he boldly announced, "fuck it, I don't even like the planet anyway." Granted that wasn't precisely the line the press office went with, but he scrapped a bunch of sensible and reasonable green initiatives and this continues to beleaguer environmental efforts. His government's U-turn put paid to a programme to insulate Britain's homes, amongst others. It also, allegedly, will cost each UK household £150 a year as of October 2022. Cheers David!

Are You Winding Me Up?

As ever, I am deeply concerned/pissed off that this teeny subset of our demographic is permitted to make all the big grown-up decisions with such horrendously far-reaching consequences. Moreover, speaking as someone who could best be described as predictably irresponsible, I'm not even sure most of those people know *how* to grown-up effectively.

All things being equal, it would seem that harnessing wind power is a good move because it's relatively quick to implement, doesn't rip through our carbon budget and once established, basically provides free energy. According to a joint study conducted by Aarhus University and the University of Sussex, the right wind farms in the right places could meet 140% of the UK and Ireland's energy needs. 140% – why the hell are we not already doing this?

I am unapologetically about to go all Pinko Commie on you. What about installing enough wind turbines (a good place to do this, as Scotland has shown, is along transport corridors where there's already a great bloody slab of tarmac impacting the views anyway) and then once the wind turbines have paid themselves out, making electricity free? A nominal fee could be levied on households that earn in excess of £70,000 in order to pay for the maintenance and upkeep of the wind turbines which would in turn create employment for people in the communities where the wind farms are cited.

Why are you so mean about rich people?

Jealousy? Spite? Coming from normal people? Who can say. Maybe it's because I'm a commoner or maybe it's because I find an energy system that penalises those with the least money a bit crass. Those who are on prepayment meters (because they have no money) pay the most (with money they are presumably supposed to crap) for the electricity they consume – this is bananas and wrong. In March 2022, the papers ran a story about how food banks were declining offers of root vegetables because people couldn't afford the energy required to cook them. Now, far be it for me to think bringing up how the English behaved in Ireland is a good idea, but just to clarify, people are too poor to eat potatoes. Is this not ringing anyone else's "Danger, Will Robinson" alarm?

Please tell me you didn't just go there with a lazy stereotype about the Irish and potatoes, tsk tsk.

The Irish diaspora is a result of people (my forebears included) fleeing conditions in their home country in the hope of finding better elsewhere. It certainly wasn't meant to end up with people living in another country where there was also a dearth of edible sodding spuds. The very food stuff that was historically the staple of people without any money is now unaffordable in Britain. Levelling up indeed. Although, there is a certain parallel that one could draw between British governments failing to care about ordinary people. 'If we can't have the colonies any more, let's recreate

Colony-Chic at home. Huzzah!' Reasonable energy use should not be a privilege for the wealthy – who are, almost without exception, wealthy because of circumstance and not because they are inherently more 'hard-working' or 'deserving.' Give the entire nation a sensible quota of free domestic energy and then implement a means tested maintenance levy on those who can afford it. Next.

Megawealth Stinks

Elon Musk is currently the richest man on Earth and famously tweeted that he is 'accumulating resources to help make life multiplanetary & extend the light of consciousness to the stars.' Personally, I think he spelt twat wrong. Megawealth has to be banned. I know that, on paper, taxation systems have this under control but, newsflash, mega wealthy people can afford very diligent accountants. Not for them the silent screams of doing your tax return online the day before the deadline and kicking yourself repeatedly for being moronic enough to think being self employed was ever a sensible notion. A simple wealth cap, above which you pay 100% tax would teach people to be content with what they have, to be more judicious in their spending and all proceeds could go to the climate crisis and humanitarian issues. Honestly, why I haven't been drafted in to solve everything, I'll never know. I would say that no one should have more than £2.5 million – and that's me being generous. Should you require further convincing, I'll remind you that Musk says he's thrilled about the global recession that's bearing down on us at time of writing because, 'it's been raining money on fools for too long.' Given that he's worth an estimated $218 billion, I'd say you're wet through, mate.

Hamster Wheels

Up and down the country 1 in 7 people pay exorbitant amounts to be members of gyms so that they can attempt to undo the ills caused by our sedentary, obesogenic and mentally taxing way of life. There are approximately 7,200 gyms in the UK which are typically full of a myriad of exercise equipment plugged into the mains which zap an awful lot of juice. I would like to propose that some clever electrical engineers invent a big dynamo-type system where you have to get pedalling on a machine to make the lights come on. Someone slogging away on the cross trainer next to you can power the running machine you're pretending to hit your personal best on. This would reduce costs for gym owners who were slammed by the pandemic as well as reducing energy consumption. (And therefore carbon emissions just in case the wind turbine team is running behind schedule.) If you have a particularly devoted set of gym attendees, we might even be in a position to put power back into the grid – perhaps discounting people's membership if they generate a certain number of kilowatts.

Emma, it's not nearly as simple as that, such mechanisms are very complex.

I'm sure but that's why we have electrical engineers – they're clever, they will easily figure it out. If they patent their idea, they will also likely make a fortune in the process. Money can be very motivating.

Also, a cursory internet search shows that there are some companies that are already delivering these sorts of products.

Yes but chop chop, scale it up, roll it out.

What, are you auditioning for Rawhide?

Stop being snippy. Granted, it's not solving our dependency on gas and oil, but it would take a chunk of power usage out of the grid and let us feel like Neo in *The Matrix*.

Woodburning Stoves

As ever, the middle classes have played a blinder here. Woodburning stoves began gaining in popularity a few years back but it is now an *absolute must have* for many middle class homes across the country and in many urban centres. Burning a renewable fuel source sounds like it ought to be a good idea but this is a spectacular balls up. Not least because people typically have a stove in carbon-spewing partnership with gas and or electric consumption within the home. I get it, I do. I lived in the woods where my only means of generating heat for warmth, cooking, drinking lots of coffee and washing was through releasing, into our atmosphere, the carbon safely stowed inside the wood's cells. Fires make us feel nice. But we have to stop placing nice before necessity. If none of the aforementioned deters you, it's worth noting that a study conducted in Sheffield found that woodburning stoves emit an awful lot of nasties into your front room. This makes me feel especially good given that I have done an awful lot of group catering on an open fire, but I guess something's got to get you.

It's worth mentioning that I'm a nemophilist. No, that's not some *deeply suspect* clownfish kink but someone who *really* loves the woods. Also known as a dendrophile, I am the sort of person who has *two* favourite trees because they are both so amazing, I can't choose between them (Yew [*Taxus baccata*] and Silver Birch [*Betula pendula*] as it happens). So, massive lady boner for trees – but they release a lot of harmful nasties when you burn them. (As would you, by the way.) In short, trees are great but they can only help us save the planet if we don't cut them down and burn them in order to create a Cottagecore atmosphere. This is going to be doubly hard for some people to let go of given that rumour has it prepayment electricity meters are going to start requiring you to stuff a kidney into the slot in order to boil a kettle. In the short term, a cheap renewable energy source sounds like a good thing but then again, so did having a toff journalist as the leader of the Tory Party.

Class is Not Taught at Eton

Just so as not to disappoint us, all centrally devised policies attempting to address climate change on a community level tend to be concocted by and aimed at middle class white people.

But you're middle class and white, Emma...

Guilty as charged, but you know, the type of middle class person who is embarrassed by being middle class because I have the decency to be aware that I don't deserve my good fortune – it was an accident of birth. (And because my antecedents had the good sense to leave Ireland to come and be servants for rich English people. Kerching.) I am, as we all are, guilty of only being able to view the world through my own lens. I try to be empathetic but it's a conscious act I have to take part in rather than it coming naturally to me – I have only lived my own life and therefore am pretty ignorant of the realities of being part of the agricultural industry, for example. On a broader scale, this creates a massive fucking problem because our country is largely run by upper middle class white boys. The Civil Service also has rather a lot to answer for in terms of representative diversity. In the first place, upper middle class white boys have a pretty stonking sense of entitlement and exceptionalism – this means, for example, that they think parties during lockdown are ok, because the Bollinger won't drink itself. In addition, I struggle to believe that a man whose wife can readily afford to voluntarily (if somewhat belatedly) pay £218 million in tax without having to sell either the North Yorkshire mansion or London crash pad, is able to cater to the needs of an electorate that may as well be from another planet. If you own more than one house, you don't really stand a cat's chance in hell of considering the struggles faced by an NHS nurse struggling to choose between heating and eating. Posh people don't relate very well to normal people – this is not me being divisive, this is fact. Most of Westminster don't know how the real world operates. Let's just pause for a moment to remind ourselves that King Charles III, darling of the contemporary environmental movement, posh Cornish biscuits, new King etc., historically sought counsel and advice from Jimmy Savile (the prolific sex criminal) on how to relate to 'ordinary people' because Savile's Leeds accent marked him as a good representative of the common man. What's really sad is that this isn't even libellous – Lord, I wish I was exaggerating here.

Denial Ain't Just a River in Egypt

At time of writing, the news that the world's richest man has withdrawn his offer for a social media giant, offers me a glimmer of hope. Increasingly, it feels as though Musk is head of *Cyberdyne Systems* and that all his machinations will lead us to ruin. Thank God, Schwarzenegger is still on the scene to kick arses and take names. Aside from Musk's absurd 'solution' to Earth's encroaching uninhabitability being for us to all upsticks to Mars, social media is a problem. Free speech is all very laudable when people are sharing advice on wearing masks in enclosed spaces and adhering to social distancing guidelines to save people's lives, but has such a potential for harm, for example, when it propagates mis-information about vaccines. Much as it chaps the arses of the scientists, people are more inclined to read something their mate shared on their timeline than they are the IPCC AR6. And boy, do people share a lot of shit. Additionally, the sheer volume of shite is as big a problem on Amazon as it is on Twitter. If you are being ecologically excellent and searching for books on climate science with which to educate yourself, you get a worrying number of 'alternative viewpoints'/400 pages of 'free speech' which all the best programming-will in the world, isn't going to eradicate. Lest we forget that NASA makes programming errors that make multi million dollar space rockets make big bangs on the surface of Mars.

Sounds a bit like you only like shouting into an echo chamber. Surely the arguments for climate change should stand up to scrutiny, interrogation and opposition?

They 100% do (but then I would say that, wouldn't I?) but, for some unknown reason, we are becoming less trusting of official messages and increasingly don't have the time or the energy to interrogate every single news story that pops up on our screens. Between Special Military Operations and people not remembering whether they had/hadn't attended parties that were/weren't allowed, we are increasingly cynical. Climate scepticism is also delightfully helpful because it removes all culpability on our parts: how can we be Earth-trashing arseholes if the planet isn't even being trashed? How on Earth do we facilitate healthy debate and dialogue on an issue that is going to need more than the input of the scientists calling us back from the edge of the crevasse caused by glacial melt and the deniers who are heavily invested in Texan oil?

Stop Electing Bellends

I have no desire to be accused of being repetitive but, we have to stop electing bellends. I really can't stress this enough. A sizeable majority of the politicians you've heard of are odious. And boy, have we heard a lot about Boris Johnson. That's not slander, defamation or me being a dick; it's just fact. There are plenty of rogue good eggs knocking about in politics, but they are emphatically the exception that proves the rule. We need better options at elections and we need to start making better choices. Quickly. We are, regrettably, dependent on politicians to scale up our good intentions to society-wide, permanent change. As David

Wallace-Wells admits, 'individual lifestyle choices do not add up to much, unless they are scaled by politics.' Balls.

And Another Thing – The Iron Age

We live in a society that judges people on *how smooth their clothes are.*

Let that sink in for a moment.

We make hefty value judgements – on the state of someone's mental health, of their domestic arrangements, their suitability for a professional role and so on, based on whether they spend time and or resources on making their clean, dry clothes look smoother.

"World hunger will have to wait – I have a tramline on my best Oxford that needs attending to."

Batshit. Our planet is dying and we burn fossil fuels and cause additional pollution to smooth out our clothes. Don't even start me on ironing water. Absolutely fucking batshit.

So, what can you do? It's simple: stop ironing. Lonely old me refusing to ever pick up an iron again isn't going to make much of a dent on a certain purveyor of ironing water or scent boosting bollocks, but if the entire country called time on what is a frankly absurd use of our precious days on Earth and we all stopped ironing there would be less water wastage, less electricity usage, fewer irons manufactured and fewer injuries related to collapsing and stowing the ironing board. I haven't had this figure fully verified but I'm pretty confident that ironing board mishaps account for at least 60% of A&E Department attendances.

We don't need smooth clothes. We're lucky we have clean clothes – let that be enough.

Toilets Are Meant to Be Dirty

When I lived in the woods, I used any quiet spot (remember naturalist, *not* naturist) for number ones and a latrine or long drop for number twos. A long drop is a long rectangular hole in the ground about as deep as the head of the spade you dig it with – think along the lines of a small grave for poos and you're close. You squat (carefully – no one wants to fall in that sort of grave) which is also incidentally much better for your bowels, do your business, wipe, burn your toilet roll and then sprinkle a bit of the dug out soil on your contribution to hyper-fertilising that trench. Safe, simple, effective and as long as the location was well chosen, doesn't pose a health risk or olfactory assault to your nearby camp.

In the UK, we flush our toilets with perfectly drinkable water. A third of the world's population does not even have access to safe drinking water – and we flush our carseys with what is an increasingly scarce and precious resource. It is not beyond the wit of man to re-plumb our houses so that we collect grey water from sinks, showers and baths and use that to flush our loos. Chartered Institute of Plumbing – I'm looking at you. Crack on.

Insulate the House You Don't Own

One of the many facets of the present climate crisis that upsets me is the assumption that everyone has autonomy over their place of residence. (To be clear, I do not as I do not own my own home – nor do I reasonably expect to in the foreseeable future. In part this is due to my life choices and in part this is due to maths.) This is largely because most of the rules in this country are created by an utterly clueless and out of touch elite. A message to said eejits: most rental tenants are not even allowed to put up a picture or change a room's paint colour without penalty – much less insulate it so their abode is more environmentally friendly. Yes, home insulation is potentially an efficient way of reducing emissions caused by home heating but policies and incentives need to reflect the reality that, as of February 2020, only 60% of British adults owned their own home. Moreover, home ownership is more concentrated amongst white Britons and over 65s. It is worth noting that home insulation isn't perfect and it depends on the house in question as to whether it will reduce your carbon footprint or potentially cause damp to develop. Fortunately, we can leave the tiny violins in their cases – 48% of the private rental sector in the UK is owned by landlords who own five or more properties. These are not retired HGV drivers trying to accrue a modest nest egg. These are substantial property portfolios and landlords who hold huge amounts of housing stock – the responsibility for upgrading them and making them more energy efficient sits squarely with them and is ripe for regulation.

Can We All Just Try to Have A Nice Time?

One of the things that really chaps my protest placard is that we continue to fail to engage people (other than softly-spoken, highly educated, white people) in discussion regarding the environment and the natural world. One of the huge drivers of this is the way in which we speak and write about the natural world. We continue to insist upon ridiculously hushed tones and conceiving of every experience as a brush with the sublime and really, it's absurd. I spent several years of my life sleeping on the floor in the woods (under a tarp [no tent] and in a sleeping bag on a roll mat) and I can assure you that nature has a pretty decent sense of humour (for a girl).

Emma, you're anthropomorphising, nature is neutral.

Nature is neutral as it pertains to meeting the needs and desires of people – it's pissing rain, you're hungry, no dice sort of neutral but nature is truly playful.

One of the things I enjoy about nature is that it amuses me. I smirk as I walk past the pigeon print (the oils in the poor bird's feathers have made the most stunning rendering, it's a thing of beauty) on the window in my lounge, I like seeing the Canada geese giving it a load of mouth to all the other birds when you go to feed the ducks and then watch them brick it as soon as a solitary swan comes along. ("Sorry Mr Swan, was just leaving Mr Swan, right you are Mr Swan.") We ought to be amused rather than expected to sit in raptured silence. One of the skills I'm trying to pass onto my kids is how to interpret and follow animal tracks and sign. Teaching them to spot the footprints of a hare (bigger than you'd think) or the slither marks of a slow worm (vanishingly rare). These moments are cute enough to enjoy with my kids but the best thing I ever 'read' from the landscape was the deer that stacked it.

Are You Sitting Comfortably?

Once upon a time, in some deciduous British woodland. I spied some deer slots (this is the name given to the deer's footprints). Almost certainly fallow (*Dama dama*) deer (not because I'm some phenomenal tracker but because there were shed loads of them in the area I was working in) and it was clearly picking its way through some really boggy ground towards the edge of a pretty stinky, slow running stream. I like to think that it fancied a drink but when it got close enough for a sniff it realised it smelled god-awful and so decided against it. The mud had other ideas though and the deer had clearly pitched arse over tit – as evidenced by the large and graceless deer arse print in the mud and the scrabbling gouges where it'd tried to get up like Bambi (how apt) on ice. We need to lighten up about nature – our gravity is putting people off. And at this point, putting people off being invested in nature is bloody irresponsible.

Domestic Issues

We have become increasingly concerned with how clean our homes are. This is not good for anyone. We really don't need to live in such immaculate homes – and I'm not just saying this because I lived in the woods and I have low standards. It's not good for our health to live in sterile environments and is possibly a contributory factor in the sharp rise in serious allergies. It's both pleasing and relaxing to learn that keeping our homes in less than magazine shoot ready condition is something to be encouraged for our own health and that of the planet. Try to buy fewer household cleaning products. Try to care less about what your house looks like. This is where children really come into their own. Perhaps we could establish a carbon off-setting scheme for kids. They trash your house rendering any amount of house pride equally futile and absurd, and you can keep the carbon points you saved on fewer cleaning products.

The Water Cycle

All sewers are connected to your kitchen tap.

I thought you were meant to be encouraging us not *to buy bottled water Emma?*

I was, I am, be quiet, please. Our water system is entirely cyclical – no water is 'created' it's just moved about and cleaned up a bit.

What about all that new water melting from the glaciers you were going on about?

That's actually old water, its state has just changed from a solid to a liquid, clever dick. Our water management system in the UK is utterly remarkable and subsequently water borne illness is very low down the list of threats to your wellbeing if you are lucky enough to live here. I am absolutely not advocating homoeopathy as a cure for anything other than relieving you of your money but we should all have a bit of a re-think about what we put into the water system. There are some scary things called forever chemicals, and whilst they may sound like a bad Emo band, they are really nasty fuckers. As per their name, they are not going anywhere and so we can't truly 'throw them away.' As ever, there's a simple solution here: simply stop manufacturing them. Government regulation is surely born for issues such as these. Also, returning to our desire to have houses like operating theatres, we ought to slash how many noxious sprays and potions we spaff all over our houses. (Or pay our cleaners to do on our behalf because we don't like breathing that stuff in.)

So now you're coming for Mrs Hinch?

Nope, and actually she is an advocate for fewer products, elbow grease and taking charge of your domestic environment – all things I can get behind and notions we might apply to the wider issue of planetary clean up.

What You Can Actually Chuffing Do:

1. Be vegan – *yeah, thanks, you already mentioned that.*
2. Stop using fabric softener – it's made from animal fat.
3. If you can afford it, have milk delivered in glass (obviously plant milk).
4. Biodegradable dog poo bags – I was shamefully late to the party on this one.
5. Raise your kids to be ecological legends – if you simply must breed – at least raise them not to be the wrong sort of people.
6. Waste less food – it's insane to fill up landfills with food that took a shit tonne of time, energy and water to produce.
7. Fly less – it puts pollutants way up in the atmosphere exacerbating their impact.
8. Buy secondhand whenever you can. It uses fewer resources and keeps thing from landfill a little bit longer.

9. Learn five non-horticultural plant names. May I suggest burdock (*Arctium lappa*) plantain (*Plantago major*) nettle (*Urtica dioica*) jack by the hedge (*Alliaria petiolata*) and goosegrass (*Galium aparine*).

10. Buy larger quantities of wine. Transporting wine in glass bottles is more carbon intensive than the comparatively lightweight plastic and cardboard of a box.

Chapter 7
God Loves a Trier

I was lucky enough to be born to an inordinately intelligent and sensible mother. She has taught me much, some of which I've even retained, but that doesn't mean I don't enjoy ripping it out of her on occasion. Along with her infamous, "can we all just *try* to have a nice time?" maxim, she was also obsessive about making us go for a wee before we left the house.

"Muuuum, I don't need a wee!"

"Just go and have a try."

And lo, most of the time, it was worth the trip.

I wish to propose something utterly unrevolutionary. How about we *try* this vegan-eating, planet-saving thing? Just go and have a try? We could call ourselves trygans or treegans? We can call ourselves anything you like so long as people dial down the cynicism a notch and, gritting my teeth even thinking this but, try to be open minded. Try to be nice. Try not to be a dick. At risk of sounding all earnest at this point in the proceedings, just imagine what could happen.

So, are we or aren't we all going vegan?

I feel I'm at fault here; there are grey areas and a lack of absolute rules which isn't especially helpful. Unfortunately, I think our food culture has to focus on a return to some balance. Balance does not look like a whole pint of milk and three portions of meat each a day. It just can't – because if we want to maintain that, Earth is done for. A few animals in areas that can't be re-wilded or crops sustainably grown may bring *some* (often exaggerated by livestock advocates) benefits for land management and fertilisation but this is a million miles away from our industrial farming model. Maybe two million miles. Realistically, we're still talking about shutting most of the livestock farms. Animal products need to become a treat, a luxury item, an occasional indulgence. For the most part, we all need to be mostly vegan. Mostly.

This is not like that point in your life when all your mates started getting married and then turned into recruitment agents for marriage, so as to have company in their misery/regrettable lifestyle choice. I promise. I want us all to give it a go because I think living is nice and we've had a go – seems fair that subsequent batches of humans get a turn too.

Vegemite and Nooch

My agent has remarked, on several occasions, that I'm like Marmite – and I'm pretty sure that he doesn't like Marmite. There are some nutrients that a vegan diet does not provide or that are harder to obtain because they are less bioavailable in plant form. Some people will find it near impossible to meet all of their nutritional needs through a totally vegan diet, many people will be absolutely fine. Given how many bunnies I've butchered, perhaps my opinion is worthless but I think there is a place for a small amount of high welfare meat, game and genuinely high welfare dairy. This is not giving credibility to the Red Tractor certification scheme (OneKind and Compassion in World Farming ranked it as the lowest in England and Scotland) which permits full time tethering of dairy cows, teeth clipping and tail docking of pigs and densely packed sheds full of broiler chickens. Cheeky Nando's anyone?

So, it sounds like you're trying to hold onto Cheddar, Emma.

Yeah, I've admitted I'm partial to cheese. Regenerative farming, inclusive of very, very small numbers of livestock has an important role to play in fixing our industrial agricultural systems but there certainly won't be enough pork chops to go around. There are other ways, vegan ways, to meet all nutritional requirements but some people may require supplementation in order to stay healthy. Marmite/Vegemite and nutritional yeast (nooch) are sources of vitamin B12 and taste good in a surprising number of dishes. So, for those of us who don't have the first clue about nutritional science, spreading some Vegemite on your toast or shaking a bit of nooch on your pasta isn't overly taxing.

So, we're living on brown paste and deactivated yeast flakes? Fantastic. Anything else we ought to roll our eyes at?

Just to remind you that Jonathan Safroen Foer also believes that, 'we cannot keep the kinds of meals we have known and also keep the planet we have known …We cannot save the planet unless we significantly reduce our consumption of animal products.' Therefore, it's a choice between chicken wings and having somewhere nice to live.

To follow are some sensible and some bonkers ideas for things we could try – it's got to be worth a shot.

Food Swaps

At time of writing, a pack of sausages, a portion of mince and 2 chicken breasts costs £11.43 from a major supermarket. How about, for one week only, not buying those 3 items but instead ordering an organic vegetable box and seeing how it pans out. At worst you might discover you really can't find anything palatable to cook with Swiss chard but at best you may find out that your head doesn't fall off if you eat less animal protein and more vegetables three times in seven days.

God, you sound like my mum and organic food is so wanky.

No actually, I sound like *my* mum but that's a good thing as she's got common sense in abundance. Organic food has been slightly unfairly aligned with privileged foodies and I think it too would benefit from a re-brand. We need to conceive of organic food being food that is grown sustainably/in a way that isn't contributing to the end of life on Earth. Also, I'm confident you don't want to eat pesticides if you can help it – it's unwise to shove a load of chemicals into your body unnecessarily. It's odd, I really thought the anti-vaxxers would have more to say on this score.

Changing Rooms

Over the last few decades, it has become very normal and aspirationally appealing for people to redecorate, *ad nauseam*, their homes. Obviously, this is mostly true of the odd 60% of Britons that own their own home and so are *allowed* to paint the lounge in sage green and refurbish the kitchen. But home decor is a growth sector of the economy and actually enjoyed buoyancy during the pandemic when most of us were stuck at home, staring at the (peeling) walls. There are two things that I consider to be wrong with this state of affairs. Firstly, it's a god-awful waste of money to keep redecorating your house because you have a man crush on that crumpet, Nick Knowles. Secondly, it's a gross waste of resources – renovations are far from environmentally friendly and almost all redecorating waste (old paint pots, stripped wallpaper, paintbrushes you couldn't be bothered to clean properly, soft furnishings you now think look a bit tired) ends up in landfill. And here's the thing with landfill – if we fill all of the land with all of our crap, we won't have anywhere nice to live, or get healthy water or food from.

Helpfully, I have a suggestion. Pick a super neutral palette of paint colours next time you *need* to redecorate. Then accessorise your house with statement pieces. (Because if we can't have fashionable interiors, then what *will* people think of us?) As I understand it, this is what people who dress well do (it won't surprise you that I don't fall into this category) – by wearing statement foundation pieces and then accenting and accessorising them. Look, I really have no business advising on things pertaining to taste or style but there'll be plenty of Pinterest ideas on the subject, I'm sure. Just please stop doing up your house every five minutes because you're bored/fancy a change. Thanks.

Diamonds Are from Heifers

So, did you know that scientists are readily able to manufacture diamonds? God, science is good. There are a couple of techniques, but one promising option is to use methane (even worse than carbon dioxide in terms of planetary warming). So, here's an idea. Why don't we establish (using some mad venture capital secured from tax avoiding offshore sources) an outfit to manufacture diamonds, big 'heirloom' ones, from methane that has been drawn down from the atmosphere (a bit like carbon capture but for cow guffs). Rich people can then purchase these 'eco diamonds' at great expense and wear them to look all sparkly at the same time as conducting some epic virtue signalling. Because whilst rich people like expensive diamonds, they also really like virtue signalling.

Yes, it will cost a lot of money to set up and is a bit batshit but do you know what really rich people also like? Batshit ideas and spending lots of money. Also, if a heap of their massive expenditure is diverted into diamond alchemy rather than super yachts, we've done the planet a massive solid. Super yachts are terrible for the planet and a remarkably reliable indicator with which to identify people who are massive arseholes that no one ever says no to. It is estimated that a fairly average superyacht, you know, nothing fancy, emits about 7,000 tonnes of carbon dioxide a year. This just should not be permissible. Being wealthy needs to cease being a licence to behave with impunity. Our lives depend upon it.

Live Aid Minus the Concord

Perhaps we too should take our cue from the birds – it's apparent that people prefer songs to science. As a child of the eighties, I grew up in the self-congratulatory glow of Live Aid. We need a new Live Aid. Rather than trendy youngsters going to festivals with single use tents and throw away wellies, why not stage a massive, planet Earth-centred gig to get everyone excited. Serve vegan food, ensure there's sustainable sleeping arrangements but let's get some bloody good acts to engage people. Obviously don't let the acts fly all over the shop (even if it is for a good cause) because that smacks of hypocrisy and you know how I brook no shit in that quarter. I also have a thing for musical theatre. Everything from music hall and vaudeville through to Lord Webber and HRH Lin Manuel Miranda. Hell, let's have a few musicals chucked in there for good measure. Cultural expressions are important and a great medium through which to educate people. I genuinely would never have known (or cared) about the bui doi (Amerasian children who were the result of unions between American soldiers and Vietnamese women during the Vietnam War) were it not for *Miss Saigon*. Admittedly, it hasn't inspired me to become an activist for this particular historic cause but it *could* have. And at least I've been made aware. Why do we scoff and sneer at the educative potential of music, musicals, films, post ecological apocalyptic youth fiction and, ahem, comedic renderings of the climate emergency?

Yeah, but they just made Don't Look Up *and no one really cared.*

Granted, despite its heavyweight ensemble cast, it wasn't quite the critical success one might have hoped for but there's still a gaping cultural hole we could fill with all sorts of wonders. Remember – *any* story that sticks. Creatives do your thing.

Wine - Coffee

As a parent to three young children, I oscillate between being over caffeinated and a bit tipsy. How the hell else am I meant to write a book at night time? Inconveniently for me, these are two particularly climate-sensitive crops and so I have a large amount of skin in this game. Anyway, I have yet another confession – I have (and adore) my coffee machine that makes yummy, mummy go-go juice. To clarify, I'm absolutely not claiming to be a Yummy Mummy™. I live in cardigans and leisure wear and have pursued writing rather than television work for good reason. But I lean heavily on coffee to ensure I love my children and don't execute people without letting them pray. My coffee machine is one of the ones that's bad for the planet because it creates waste through its single use aluminium pods. I'm not lying to make myself sound better here – we really do take ours to the local retailer to recycle them but I'm not convinced they are all processed as their marketing materials so angelically claim. My husband and I have repeatedly tried to find a better way to drink coffee. And when I say better,

I mean 'tasting exactly the same with no additional labour, inconvenience or expense.' Thus far, we've baulked at the cost of a low waste, bean-to-cup machine because I'm tight. It's on my to-do-list, I promise.

N.B. – We can all eco audit our lives and homes and make a mental note of things we can do differently/better/give up because you're sick of feeling crap about yourself. I have a number of items on my own list. I'm working on it.

Sip Sip

I don't like my wine glasses. They're a funny shape – too close to a cocktail glass and weirdly hard to hold (when you're hitting the contents with intent) but I've resolved not to replace them for the sake of my silly dislike of them. Naturally, as a consequence, I haven't broken one in years. In truth, I long for one of those large bulbous sorts that attractive Californians drink from in their spotless kitchens after a taxing day as an attorney at law. Granted, most of my wine drinking is done after a day of raising my own children and wearing leggings but such is life. I have tried to compensate for my coffee failings by drinking from ugly wine glasses. Now that is ecological sacrifice for you. (Done badly – mock me, judge me and don't emulate me.)

Deliveroo Us from Evil

So unless you've been living under a rock/in the woods, you're probably aware that Deliveroo is a very successful food delivery service. Successful enough that they aren't even upset that it's widely known they use 'self-employed contractors' to help build and grow their highly profitable business. Just in case you've never been a self-employed contractor, it means that you get no sick pay, no holiday pay and your 'I am not your employer' doesn't have to make any National Insurance contributions on your behalf because they came to make money, not to prop up the NHS, thank you very much. Typically, these sorts of workers are at the mercy of unreliable and antisocial hours, low pay and little to no job security. Oh, and these ones have to maintain a bike and consume enough calories themselves to bring you your dim sum in a hurry – really, capitalism has so much to recommend it. At least it has a lovely brand origin story: it was co-founded by Will Shu, a former investment banker with Morgan Stanley and a recipient of an MBA who ran it out of the London flat (he probably owned, in Chelsea, no less) for a year while starting up – classic rags to filthy riches tale, real salt of the earth. He earns about £600,000 a year in addition to his share payouts so that makes it an extra cool way to treat his (not) employees.

Aside from their questionable employment practices, Deliveroo is indicative of the way the food industry feeds (see what I did there?) an unhealthy and unsustainable food culture and system. It isn't remotely normal to tap a few times on a smartphone screen and have duck gyoza magically appear at your place of work with a side of squid rings inside 15 minutes BECAUSE WE'RE NOT WIZARDS! We aren't meant to be able to procure so much food, so quickly. One of two things happens – we eat too much and get fat or we eat only some of it and the rest gets wasted. Both are supremely unhelpful and the latter is a major driver of our sticky climate problem. Of course, no one wants to eat their stale and lacklustre sandwich they should have made at home at the crack of Satan but that's life/lunch. And don't get me started on the packaging waste it creates. What's wrong with a stained, old Tupperware leaching BPA into your leftover stir fry, eh? When did we all become such insufferable food snobs?

Why Can Some Families Cook?

I can cook.

Yeah, you said. At least twice.

Sure, I'm not applying for Masterchef anytime soon (although I'd definitely do melting chocolate puddings, just to be a dick) but I am able to feed myself and my family, reasonably good fare without too much stress. I have worked in catering but there are a number of reasons I have acquired the skills to feed people. My Nana (my great grandmother) was in service. This is an aspiring middle class, euphemistic term for having been a servant. One of her duties as a servant was to run the kitchen and, probably with the help of Mrs Beeton, she established herself as a brilliant cook. Not a wanky 'I need plaudits for my ego, chef,' but a cook. Once she was married, she obviously had to hand in her notice because our society was a bit uncool about female employment in those days, but she cooked brilliant fare for her own family, who she taught to cook in turn. This familial knowledge filtered down to me and my cousins – most of whom have a good grasp of the culinary arts. This is, as ever, an accident of birth. I did not earn this knowledge, but I am able to use it to keep myself and my children fed with nutritious food that I also select to have a lower environmental impact. This is a privilege I benefit from and one that we need to extend to everyone. We need to reinstate a value in cooking for yourself and your loved ones – and not the show-off fare of dinner parties but the everyday, normal 'home food' that's inexpensive, filling and doesn't tear the arse out of the environment.

The Body Electric

I still remember the gentle hiss of my mum's Braun curling tongs. They pre-dated straighteners and were lauded for being portable and enabling you to touch up your eighties power perm on the move. The sound of the ignition switch

– it never lit first time, the hiss of the gas canister held worryingly close to your face and eyes, the smell of slightly singed hair – we had it so good. We are more energy hungry than ever. The West is particularly ravenous in this regard. Wind farming is a sensible way to meet our current and future power needs but actually, we need to start reducing our energy usage because even if we can use renewable energy to meet all of our present power needs, as we rapidly phase out fossil fuels, we will need more electrical energy to heat our homes and power our transportation.

I have become a bit of a kitchen gadget collector. I have a bread machine, a rice cooker, a slow cooker and a toasted sandwich maker. These all run on mains power and I also have a gas oven and hob. This really isn't great. Firstly, it's not all that ideal in terms of my children breathing indoors small particulate pollution but it's also a relatively inefficient use of energy. My rice cooker can cook (superior) rice to me boiling it to death, white girl style, on the hob. (My other sister-in-law is Chinese and she just does not understand what rice did to white people to make them hate it so much.) Some gadgets and appliances can save energy or make more efficient use of it. Moreover, the sooner we go hard on the wind farm front, mains electricity will actually be a pretty green source of power and British Gas will have to have a re-think on its brand identity. Switching to energy efficient devices that you use and keep for a long time (so as to 'pay out' their embedded carbon costs) isn't the worst idea. It's better for example, to make a loaf of bread in an energy efficient machine as opposed to buying loaves in plastic and letting them go mouldy in your bread bin.

Got Wood?

One of my most prized possessions is a copy of *Wayside and Woodland Trees* by Edward Step. It's a field guide for tree nerds and it's beautiful. The cover leaf bears the epigraph, 'Of all man's works of art, a cathedral is greatest. A vast and majestic tree is greater than that.' Henry Ward Beecher was a clergyman who was keen on both the abolition of slavery *and* adultery – as in he delighted in adultery and didn't want to abolish it. What a lad. I mentioned earlier that I have a thing for trees. I'm not especially prone to hugging them but I like woodland, wooden things, things that look, smell and taste like wood. I'm going to take the liberty of being embarrassingly earnest; I just love trees. Being amongst trees makes me feel really calm, safe and markedly less anxious than I am in any other environment. This sounds like I'm unhinged but deciduous trees (the ones that spend the winter naked) release a range of chemicals called phytoncides and these volatile compounds are fantastically clever. Much has been made (and mocked) in the press in recent years over forest bathing but my less flashy, lifelong obsession of 'going for a walk in the woods' seems to have some rigorous scientific backing. These compounds may even be able to reduce the incidence of cancer in human cells. When I said I'm not a hugger, that's not strictly true. I do like to touch trees; I like the way they feel under my fingertips and…

This totally sounds like that weird kink you were on about.

So sue me. Maybe it is a kink (although it seems pretty pedestrian given what a lot of people get up to) but you should try it and see how you respond. My favourite tree to touch? It's the hornbeam (*Carpinus betulus*) and its bole (the trunk) remind me of an elephant's legs. They seem somehow muscular with an ancient and unyielding strength.

This is sounding dangerously close to a Regency romp.

Ok, it's a bit weird. But appreciating and taking pleasure from things that are soothing, don't harm anyone or anything and are free, should perhaps be encouraged rather than derided.

As an aside, it would be really useful if men would stop murdering women and dumping their bodies in woodland as it's really putting people, especially women, off spending time outdoors, especially alone. I have spent hundreds of nights sleeping alone on the forest floor and the only thing I ever feared was other people. Ok, and sometimes hornets. It's the only bug that gives me the willies. They aren't actually aggressive, but it *feels* pretty aggressive when you're wearing a head torch at night (they are attracted to light) and you happen to have set up a camp next to an oak tree with a bloody great nest in it. Back to not murdering people.

Wild, desolate places should be somewhere to enjoy and draw solace from – not to fear that you'll be the next grisly statistic. Guys – have a word.

Trees are not only beautiful and majestic beasts, they also have a huge part to play in helping us mop up some of this mess. They can draw down and sequester carbon through photosynthesis, they prevent soil erosion, keep temperatures lower, prevent flooding, provide habitats for animals and insects but this is contingent on us not cutting them down and not dicking around with the global thermostat any more, thus exposing them to unfavourable conditions and making them prone to disease. We are expected to lose 80% of Britain's ash trees (*Fraxinus excelsior*) in the near future thanks to ash dieback (*Hymenoscyphus fraxineus*) – a non native fungus which kills ash trees. As with many fungi, they enjoy warm and humid conditions – which are set to increase with warmer and wetter summers. We still don't really know the extent of the damage of losing an entire species from British woodland, but we can safely assume it will be bad news for all of the insects, microbes, birds, fungi and mammals for whom it's an integral part of their ecosystem.

According to the Woodland trust, a young, mixed woodland can lock in 400+ tonnes of carbon dioxide per hectare. This has enormous potential for good – and makes me happy as, you know, I love trees. That being said, the level of reforestation required to make a dent in this thing is huge – impractically so. Only 13% of the UK's land has tree cover – whereas the average in that *awful* geopolitical institution we insisted on leaving is 37%. They are reintroducing wolves too, which I think we can all agree, is fucking cool. It's also important to take, with a massive pinch of salt, claims by companies off-setting their carbon emissions by planting a couple of saplings. A sapling does not have the carbon-sucking impact that is touted – it has that potential – and we need off-setting to be much more comprehensive than that.

The scale of the reforestation required in Britain alone is a bit daunting. The Woodland Trust estimates that we need to plant another 1.5 billion hectares of woodland (and it has to be of the right species in the right place – there is no point planting Alders [*Alnus glutinosa*] which like to have their feet wet, on some arid hillside) which is about the same size as Yorkshire.

That's an awful lot of trees Emma.

It really is but it's only a fraction of the ones we cut down to make things like the beams of Salisbury cathedral (still holding the roof up) and HMS Victory (which was built from more than 5,500 oak trees) so we can manage, I'm sure. Also, of all the things to be resistant towards, trees are an odd pick. No one is suggesting we bulldoze your house so that we can plant a tree there and, like much of the climate emergency, there is a sense of urgency here – in an ideal (but still dreadful for lots of people) world – these trees would have been already been planted and getting on with the job of saving our lives.

Tree Love Lasts Forever

The engineer John Smeaton's lighthouse designs are based on the shape of an oak tree. Trees only tend to go to sea as boats but arboreal engineering saves our lives in more ways than one.

I thought you said lifeforms shouldn't have to be useful to us to justify their existence…

Not to me they don't – remember I'm the weird tree lady, but there are also a number of important medical applications of trees and plants – which would also be lost if we hit the UK's Climate Change Commitee's planning recommendation of 4 degrees of warming. I live next to a farm that grows medicinal poppies and I was mightily grateful for morphine when my appendix went. The delicate flowers of the opium poppy (*Papaver somniferum*) will not be a priority crop if we're diddling about at a 4 degree temperature increase. Plants and trees give us numerous medications – the heart medication Digoxcin is derived from foxgloves (*Digitalis*), there is a brace of banging cancer drugs from yew trees (*Taxus baccata*) and willow (*Salix*) is the original source of aspirin.

Dead Oaks' Society

Beyond the immediately extractive usefulness of trees and plants, they also know a thing or two about living symbiotically. We would do well to brush up on what this means in terms of both ecology and our human communities. Trees 'talk' to each other through the mycorrhizal network in the soil and through chemical releases above ground.

Does that mean that unholy weirdness in The Happening *by M Night Shyamalan could actually happen?*

Where trees begin releasing a neurotoxin that causes people to commit suicide? Yes and no. It probably depends on how much we continue to upset the trees.

Vampire Devices

These are electrical appliances that we leave plugged into the mains which draw power, even when they are on standby. Experts are encouraging us, both for the sake of our battered bank balances and the unnecessary waste of electrical energy, to turn everything off at the socket (alright, *Dad*) when we aren't using it. However, as with many eco-solutions, this advice tanks pretty spectacularly with real world application. Sigh. Being able to switch everything off at the wall depends entirely on circumstance. For example, my washing machine is plugged into a mains socket behind the washing machine and under my kitchen counter. Obviously, I am not going to risk a hernia dragging the great beast out every single time my husband wants to use it, and again after he's finished doing all the laundry. Consider this a push back to housebuilders, electricians, manufacturers – give us appliances that don't suck juice and a practical means of managing their power usage.

Plastic Fantastic

When are we going to admit it? Plastic is really fucking convenient. Today, I asked my four-year-old what we could do to save the planet. Her reply was to, "fish all the plastic bottles out of the sea." Ouch. We use a hell of a lot of plastic – *we* being me personally and *us* as a species. Even though we know we shouldn't. We need to stop using so much plastic. Recently, researchers found microplastic particles in an unborn baby's placenta – and those placenta smoothies probably taste pretty rank as it is. There is an absolute monstrosity of plastic waste bobbing about in the sea called the Great Pacific Garbage Patch – it's very nearly an archipelago of really vile plastic crap and microplastic slurry just sitting there reminding us of how much we suck. Hugh and Anita were spot on – we all really need to use less plastic, much less, and anything we do use must be recyclable and actually get recycled. This does not mean shipping it to shithole countries so that we don't have to feel bad about it any more. It means using much, much less virgin plastic and recycling what we simply can't get round/find too inconvenient to do so. Because our addiction to plastic is an addiction to convenience – but a climate apocalypse will be even more inconvenient than having to use our stained old Tupperware rather than cling film for our sarnies.

Russian Trolls – Stupid is *and* Stupid Does

In the potentially post-apocalyptic near future, Vladimir Putin may be attributed with both starting World War Three and hastening our planet's ecological demise. Great day at the office, Vlad. At the time of writing, Putin's three day 'special military operation' is entering its fourth month. Placing aside, for a moment, the destruction of a sovereign nation and the murder of its civilians, Europeans who were already facing deeply harmful cost of living crises after the pandemic, are now staring down the (Russian issue) barrel of an energy crisis. Fossil fuels have long required fluffy, democratic countries to flex and bend their stance on human rights because when you need to buy oil, who cares if they let women drive. Russia's insistence that everyone who buys their oil and gas pays for it in Roubles is both an attempt to shore up its sanctions-hit economy and to throw its weight around in the European neighbourhood. Admittedly, threatening nuclear war also falls under this category too but the energy crisis pertains slightly more to our beloved vegans.

The understandable but (no sugar coating here) *wrong* strategy to build more coal plants, re-open the pits and frack all over the place is twice stupid. Not only does this continue pumping carbon into the atmosphere, chomping though our carbon budget faster than a climate change facilitated plague of desert locusts, having invested a load of money in renovating and rebuilding fossil-fuel energy infrastructure for this 'short term fix,' how enthusiastic do you think the policy makers are going to be about retiring them five minutes later? We have to completely revamp the entire energy system. We are talking about getting the energy sector's very own Auntie Gok in to sort this hot mess out. Otherwise, we continue to be tottering, inebriated, down a cobbled High Street in perspex stilettos, just before midnight. It's going to get ugly.

Be More Like Noel Fitzpatrick

Whilst one doesn't dare idolise anyone these days for fear of them promptly being embroiled in some sort of gross sexual misconduct scandal, I think idolising Noel Fitzpatrick, also known as the Bionic Vet, is a safe move. He is a veterinary expert in helping animals for whom euthanasia would be the more obvious choice. I would like to be friends with him firstly because he seems to have a pretty abundant access to puppies and secondly because he seems like a really nice human. None of us are perfect – in any sense. I wrote a whole bloody book about saving the planet and yet I'm doing a remarkably ineffective job of actually helping. None of us are saints – now there is a sliding scale here – on occasion I'm a crap wife, daughter, friend, colleague, neighbour and road user (I will see how much therapy my children require before I add mother to this list) but I haven't got a not-so-secret child abuse racket in a national broadcasting organisation and I didn't attend any parties during any of the lockdowns.

Humanity is going to have a rough time of it over the coming decades – even with the projected best case scenarios we are all going to experience vast changes. Much of this is going to be out of our control but I would like to make a plea for trying to be good neighbours to each other – both in a local and global sense. We all live here, some of us in closer proximity, but we can ease the burden of the challenges to some a tiny bit if we help each other out where we can. Our neighbourhoods also have wild residents and anything we can do to make their lives a bit easier, might help a bit. As Ma says in *On the Banks of Plum Creek* when she's not being horrendously racist about Native American people, 'there is nothing in the world so good as good neighbours.' Sure, she was a bigot but Ma still understood the importance of good neighbours (unlike The BBC and Channel 5). The majority of us need to stop being so selfish and start being more community minded – both in a local and global sense.

What You Can Actually Chuffing Do:

1. Cancel your superyacht order.
2. Put pan lids on when you're cooking. Yes, it means scrabbling around in the back of, what my husband affectionately refers to as 'the death cupboard,' but it reduces heat (and therefore energy) loss by 20%, so get scrabbling.
3. If you have any outside space, Heath Robinson yourself a washing line and use wooden pegs – they actually work better and don't shatter from exposure to the elements and create millions of microplastics.
4. Be a good neighbour to your neighbours.
5. Be a garden slob and don't strim, mow and weed kill the whole thing within an inch of its life. Let it all hang out so nature has somewhere to Netflix and chill.
6. Please, please don't be a bellend and drop litter.
7. Do a litter pick – there are plenty of bellends that walk amongst us. I gave my kids litter pickers as a present and they love running about the place with a bucket for collecting recycling and one for rubbish. Tires them out and cleans up the planet – full house.
8. Don't have a coffee machine that creates single use, aluminium coffee pod waste.
9. Don't use insecticides in your home – a few ants aren't going to kill you but an insect apocalypse might.

10. Try to reduce your light pollution – night time lighting really dicks about with nature's fragile balance.

Chapter 8
Anthropocene Realities

Anthropocene is a scientific euphemism to describe the period of time that man has been on Earth properly screwing things up. We all know what a nature nerd Charles Darwin, the famed naturalist and biologist was. What a loser. He was, however, famously right about a lot of things which people thought were impossible/improbable/batshit at the time he was working. He also never actually said, 'it is not the strongest of the species that survive, nor the most intelligent, but the one most responsive to change,' which is a shame for all of the people who already have that tattooed in Sanskrit across their ribcages. So, even though it's not actually something he wrote, I like to think it's something he'd find the sense in. Digging our leather heels into the drying edge of the peat bog is not the smart or the right thing to do here. Life on Earth is changing and we can either feel resentful of those changes or we can shush our noise and get on with them.

Jenga is the oft-employed analogy to illustrate ecosystem collapse, but I think a more apt one is the concept of us all continuing to haphazardly stack piles of shit adjacent to the fans. Kill the insects, the birds die and we have no crop pollinators or decent decomposers, then plant life is screwed, then small mammals, my beloved dog and the rest of us in quick succession.

Yes, but Chernobyl recovered really quickly…

Correct – nature is surprisingly plucky and resilient and the site around the Chernobyl plant has dumbfounded us with its regeneration. However, that was only one (albeit dramatically catastrophic) impact. The ecological warfare we're unleashing is more complex and frankly, a good deal more thorough than a nuclear meltdown. In this instance we're talking about denuded and diminishing habitats, warming temperatures, chemical disruptions (deliberate: pesticides, inadvertent: chicken shit run-off) freak weather, land clearance, water shortages, soil erosion. I could, truly, sadly, bleakly go on.

Eco Anxiety

Being aware that it's very fashionable to self-diagnose these days and not being someone who likes to even flirt with being 'on trend,' I may regret this but, I think I have eco anxiety. Luckily, I have my favourite whipping boy at the ready: a recent study found that it's specifically governments' inaction that is leading to people feeling 'a bit worried' about their futures and whether they'll actually have one. Understandably, these sorts of existential crises put a bit of a downer on Earth Day and could be lessened if we had policy makers who at least pretended to give a damn. (Earth Day is an annual event to try to persuade us to all notice that the planet is dying. Much like the Eurovision Song Contest, it seems to come around more than once a year. Although I should be less sniffy about Eurovision as they are markedly better at getting people excited about attending/bringing nations together for a common aim.) It seems a bit like paying your taxes twice that the effects of climate change are injurious to mental health as are the anxieties surrounding impending extinction level events – sort of the opposite of Non Dom Status where you don't pay any tax at all.

Greta the Great

I obviously couldn't write a whole book on climate change and vegans and not mention the person who is probably best-known in both spheres. At the risk of fan-girling, she's a complete wonder, a true luminary. She saw something outrageous and took action at great personal cost – I'll remind you that as a person with Asperger's syndrome, she finds public speaking, hectic environments and a total lack of routine and privacy hellish. She also managed to get under the skin of two of the most appalling humans on the planet and I'd give the girl a lifetime supply of chickpeas for that alone. Similarly, to other activists in this climate arena, she subjects herself to slander, ridicule and the complete erosion of her right to be a private citizen because she's nice and because she cares. This simply does not compute in the world of politics and self-serving celebrity. It makes no sense goddammit! Scratch the fan girl thing. She is an inspiration. She is what we need more of. What we need less of is the former Floridian Governor, now a US Senator, 'Red Tide Rick' Scott who banned the words 'climate change' and 'global warming' from state documents. This nonsense has to stop. Despite the fact that Greta apparently cannot conceive of ecological problems and any potential solutions being 'complicated and complex' ("man see country, man invade country, ugg"), she has inspired millions and millions of the humans who are going to have to live this shit that something can be done. Giving up is not an option – for Greta or for any of us and her example is something that even I won't take the piss out of.

Eco Therapy

Conveniently, there is something that we can do to help tackle eco (and other forms of) anxiety. Eco therapy has various names and guises (and price points depending on how good the marketing is) but it is basically spending time outside and not in a manmade environment. Also, as much as people are trying to make it fashionable, 'stepping out to get some air' has been a crisis management strategy since forever. More scientifically speaking, trees release phytoncides which are a free and abundant wonder chemical. These have been shown to have a positive effect on the immune system, blood pressure, lung capacity and even the elasticity of arteries. Positive forest experiences are more common in deciduous forests – as opposed to coniferous forests – which is how I feel. Broadleaf deciduous woodland feels like coming home to me.

You did live *in the woods…*

Well yes, but perhaps I was able to do that in all my fiercely diminutive glory because it felt like a safe and happy place to me. I couldn't have done it if I was stressed out by my immediate surroundings. This is despite the fact that, as I mentioned, my favourite place to hang out is also the preferred location for rapists and murderers – perhaps not an obvious choice for a lone female. I did almost always walk around with a knife, axe and saw tucked into my belt too – perhaps this deterred the wackos and emboldened me. Here are a couple of tips to ensure your eco therapy has the desired effect.

How to Be Outside and Have a Nice Time for Your Mental Health – Even When It Isn't Sunny:

A waterproof is important but never underestimate how miserable you can feel with a wet face. If your body is nice and dry, it's a small comfort if rain is streaming into your eyes. A hat with a peak keeps your face dry and your spirits up.

If it's really pouring, seek refuge under a tree – yew trees (*Taxus baccata*) are great for this – it's a truly ethereal experience and it's bizarrely more cosy than being in a building. Trust me.

Listen – put your phone away and take your headphones out for five minutes and just listen. You won't hear any insects because their numbers are dwindling but with any luck, you'll hear some birds.

Haters Gonna Hate

It's easy to mock the afflicted, and Americans (the nation that won't ban guns but will happily ban a woman's right to choose – cool) but we need to tear the arses out of people who deny/outright lie about climate change. This is doubly important if people are in positions of power and responsibility, as unlikely as these figures might be as role-models, what they say does have political and persuasive capital and they must be silenced to let the clever people speak. Granted, the scientific community isn't as charismatic as Piers Morgan spaffing off about what an incisive journalistic mind he has but with a little coaxing and the right platform, scientists might be allowed to save us all.

Parents need to stop excusing their climate-damaging behaviours as being for the betterment of your children's lives. If you have decided to breed (and many people are so concerned they have actively opted out of having families), you have a responsibility to leave the world in the best possible condition for your children. You don't hotbox your car and smear kebab grease all over the seats the night before you take it to the used car dealership for valuation, you great twonk.

Rationing Fun

Only you could possibly come up with something like this.

Hear me out. There was a time (when Boomers weren't alive, despite their pretence to the contrary) when Britain wasn't so precious about behaving in a certain way for the greater good, to benefit people other than themselves. What about having individual or household carbon budgets? This isn't an idea I can claim credit for – although you can probably have guessed I'd be on board for some self-flagellation by now. Mike Berners-Lee has proposed a 5 tonne per year lifestyle in his updated *How Bad are Bananas?* and you'd be pretty devastated at how quickly you razz through 5 tonnes of carbon. My own version is a little less fluffy, individual responsibility, and a little more cool, global governmental body mandated points system. Think of it like Weight Watchers but without the fat-shaming and profiting from society's unattainable beauty standards.

You like to fly 7 times a year? Cool. You can't drive when you're not on holibobs.

Enjoy getting your nails did, tiny individual portions of cheese and fast fashion. Cool. You won't be able to buy more than your point-permitting allocation of meat.

Had too many kids and need a van to cart them around because nobody wants your litter of children on the bus? Cool. You will all need to go vegan.

This sounds like a Gilead-esque nightmare.

Women not being able to have universal access to abortions, gay and trans people being subjected to conversion therapy and rich twats hiding all of their money in offshore tax havens such as Jersey and the British Virgin Islands, *that's* Gilead/half the states in the Union. An ecological points system is a sensible and proportionate response and has the potential to affect scaled behavioural change.

Yes, but those rich twats will just buy/bribe/steal their way to more points to continue living their utterly ridiculous lifestyles.

Of course they will – but at least it will be obvious and we can all be judgemental and feel morally superior when we're eating our parsimonious and planet-friendly turnip salads. It would also make it easier to identify assets that are avoiding taxation because if you're sunning yourself in your weekend pad in Biarritz after hopping off your private jet, it's going to be a bit obvious when the rest of the world are living like the Amish. Well hopefully not quite like the Amish. I'm actually quite fond of electricity. Wealth inequality has to be tackled if we are to successfully halt the decline of our planet's health and it will be much easier to do so if some people have a really bling buggy parked outside their homestead.

Politicians Need to Think About Future Voters

Peddling the perpetual nonsense of 'I don't think the British people want to be nannied and told what to do/buy/eat' should stop. Firstly, the notion of half of Westminster having even the foggiest idea what the rest of us think really does stretch the bounds of credulity. Secondly, most of us are actually quite happy to follow instructions/accept guidance for behaviour change/think of the greater good and make modest sacrifices for others. It is only those who are rotten apples who cannot conceive of other people being really decent bits of fruit, once you wash the pesticide off us. Moreover, the British people demonstrated a remarkably high tolerance for following the draconian rules during the pandemic. Unlike some people we could mention.

Full Up Like a Landfill

Well managed landfill sites capture a good deal of the carbon they emit. Apparently. Throwing away things that emit methane has to stop. Even lobbing some artwork from your kid that you didn't ask for in the bin emits methane as it decomposes. For those of us who are able, we must recycle diligently. Really diligently. For those of us who manage municipal recycling schemes, they must manage them diligently. Or I'm getting my slipper out.

Tears For my Fears

In addition to nature and books, I love music. I grew up listening to some excellent sounds and as a child of the eighties and I have a soft spot for Tears for Fears. To follow are some things we can jolly well do without.

Hobby Aviationists (I'm talking to you)

I am lucky enough to live both under the London Heathrow flight path and near a local air strip. Aviation gets two slippers on the back of the legs because whilst burning fossil fuels is immediately bad for the locals who have to breathe in the fumes, spaffing fossil fuels at high altitudes is even worse because of the atmospheric composition being different at high altitudes – the science is complex but by 'complex,' read, bad and worse than burning that same fuel at ground level.

"But I like flying for pleasure, it's my hobby."

Seriously? *Seriously?* We are marching towards the apocalypse but we're all sentimental and indulgent about a bunch of old, rich people who 'just love flying' and spent a house deposit on getting their pilot's licence? Come on!

I hereby ban nonsense self-indulgence.

Oranges and Lemons (Come on)

Arbitrary fresh food quantities – who decided that apples should be sold in packs of six, peppers packs of three and avocados, two? There are no two households who consistently eat satsumas at the same rate – it's bonkers and a very simple solution is to force supermarkets to sell fresh produce loose. Not only would this reduce wastage but it would also reduce the amount of 'Recycle at larger stores' plastic that many multiple items are sold in. Oh, and they'll save money. Win, win, win.

I think you'll find, Emma, that many products are just sold by weight. And 1 kg of onions weighs the same if it's composed of 4 whoppers or 7 teeny alliums.

Yes, clever dick, but weight is no less arbitrary than counting courgettes out. Make people behave like adults and buy what they can reasonably expect to need and use. Of course, absolute rules are easier to follow than subtle judgement calls requiring nuanced decision making. In short, we are going to be expected to behave like grown-ups and whilst that's not really what we signed up for, it's what's coming.

The End (May Well Be Nigh)

So, we have come to the end of what is an amusingly bleak tale and yes, you've seen that I am the very model of a modern eco criminal. But you probably are too, and nobody likes your ugly finger pointing. I want to do better, and I will continue to do better because my kids and yours (even if they're noisy and really annoying) deserve better than a shitty, short life cleaning up my mess. We are never going to live an impact-free life that doesn't leave behind anything but wanky footprints and ill-advised tattoos – I should know, I have several, but we need to do better, much better.

The Headlines: It's a big deal. It's our fault. We can and must do something about it. It's that hard and that simple. As Rob Percival reminds us, 'our diets will need to change. We will need to eat much less meat. This is not a vegan conspiracy.' It might feel like a vegan conspiracy but if anything, they're actually proving helpful. We are (too) worried about upsetting people. Time to take another leaf out of the vegans' playbook – they really couldn't give a rat's arse about who they upset. Maybe we all need to be more vegan in this regard too because, as Oliver Milman says, 'action on climate change will benefit just about everything, everywhere.' Everything, everywhere being better? Yeah, that sounds like it would appeal to most people. Going mostly/usually/as much as you can vegan is a pretty easy way to have a big impact without having to go and say, dig a long drop in the woods. Joining in with saving the planet is not quite the misery-pact that you might imagine of veganism either. There will be good days worthy of bragging about on social media and then there will be days when you have a freezer dinner of bean burgers, chips and onion rings – nobody's perfect.

But get trying.

Lots of love,

The Girl who Shat in the Woods

What You Can Actually Chuffing Do:

1. Fewer presents – less buying unwanted crap for friends and family. Switch your plastic tape for some recyclable stuff and use recycled paper in which to wrap the meaningful and thoughtful gifts you simply must give.
2. Make a meal plan – it will save you time and money from impulse buys at the supermarket and can help you easily reduce your food waste.
3. Give grief to anyone who sends you junk mail or hands you marketing materials. We don't need more paper ending up in landfill, releasing methane as it rots.

4. Recycle all junk mail and marketing materials that you get.

5. If you have a hankering for meat, try game or roadkill for a lower ecological impact.

6. Don't be so squeamish – fresh roadkill was alive a lot more recently than something killed last week in an abattoir.

7. Don't buy air-freighted food – please.

8. Don't buy bottled water, for the love of God. Just don't.

9. A good old fashioned bed airing (folding your duvet back in half to allow your shed skin cells to diffuse a bit) will enable you not to feel obliged to wash your bed sheets every other day.

10. Wash on cold. Heating water chomps through energy. Saves money, saves the planet for your grandbabies – win!

Bibliography

How Bad Are Bananas? – Mike Berners-Lee. 2020 Profile Books.

The Mad Farmer Poems: Manifesto: The Mad Farmer Liberation Front – Wendell Berry. 2011 Shoemaker & Hoard.

The Way Home – Mark Boyle. 2019 Oneworld Publications.

What We Need To Do Now: For a Zero Carbon Future – Chris Goodall. 2020 Profile Books.

Feeding Britain: Our Food Problems and How to Fix Them – Tim Lang. 2020 Pelican.

How Are we Going to Explain This? Our Future on a Hot Earth – Jelmer Mommers. 2020 Profile Books.

Regenesis – George Monbiot. 2022 Allen Lane.

The Insect Crisis: The Fall of the Tiny Empires that Run the World – Oliver Milman. 2022 Atlantic Books.

The Meat Paradox – Rob Percival. 2022 Little, Brown.

Hope in Hell: A Decade to Confront the Climate Emergency – Jonathon Porritt. 2020 Simon & Schuster.

We Are the Weather: Saving the Planet Begins at Breakfast – Jonathan Safran Foer. 2020 Penguin.

Uninhabitable Earth: A Story of the Future – David Wallace-Wells. 2019 Penguin.

Suggested Reading List

There is No Planet B – Mike Berners-Lee. 2021 Cambridge University Press.

Uninhabitable Earth: A Story of the Future – David Wallace-Wells. 2019 Penguin.

Braiding Sweetgrass – Robin Wall Kimmerer. 2020 Penguin.

We are the Weather: Saving the Planet Begins at Breakfast – Jonathan Safran Foer. 2020 Penguin.

Small Farm Future – Chris Smaje. 2020 Chelsea Green.

Field Work – Bella Bathurst. 2021 Profile Books.

All We Can Save – Ed. Ayana Elizabeth Johnson & Katharine K. Wilkinson. 2020 Penguin Random House.

Hope in Hell: A Decade to Confront the Climate Emergency – Jonathon Porritt. 2020 Simon & Schuster.

Losing Earth: The Decade we Could Have Stopped Climate Change – Nathaniel Rich. 2020 Picador.

The Future We Choose – Christiana Figueres & Tom Rivett-Carnac. 2021 Manilla Press.

How are we Going to Explain This? Our Future on a Hot Earth – Jelmer Mommers. 2020 Profile Books.

No One is Too Small to Make a Difference – Greta Thunberg. 2019 Penguin.

Eating Animals – Jonathan Safran Foer. 2011 Penguin.

Feeding Britain: Our Food Problems and How to Fix Them – Tim Lang. 2020 Pelican.

How to Avoid a Climate Disaster – Bill Gates. 2021 Penguin.

What we Need to do Now: For a Zero Carbon Future – Chris Goodall. Chris Goodall. 2020 Profile Books.

Feral – George Monbiot. 2014 Penguin.

Regenesis – George Monbiot. 2022 Allen Lane.

This Changes Everything – Naomi Klein. 2015 Penguin.

The Meat Paradox – Rob Percival. 2022 Little, Brown.

Silent Earth: Averting the Insect Apocalypse – Dave Goulson. 2022 Vintage.

The Hidden Life of Trees – Peter Wohlleben. 2017 William Collins.

Back to Nature – Chris Packham. 2021 Two Roads.

How Bad Are Bananas? – Mike Berners-Lee. 2020 Profile Books.

The Insect Crisis: The Fall of the Tiny Empires that Run the World – Oliver Milman. 2022 Atlantic Books.

For a much better explanation of how big businesses are massive dicks, do read *Butler to the World* – Oliver Bullough. 2022 Profile Books.

Acknowledgements

Getting published is like falling in love; everyone says no to you at first, and then, when you finally get an offer, you cling to it in a desperate and unbecoming manner. As all (honest) writers will concede, it takes more than a village to raise a book from a pile of wood pulp. I owe special thanks to my husband Tom, mum Mary, Auntie Sheila and Uncle Peter and the rest of my long-suffering (hugely embarrassed, can't even brag about my book at Mass) relatives. To my friends Candace, Lauren, Sharkey, Ellie, Kim, Char, Sarah, Alice, Tess, Rachel, Jack, Radhika, James, Hugh, Charlotte, Rob, Bea, Margaret. To Tanja – thanks for being cool about that thing I thought. To Ray, for giving me a job. To all of my lovely woods comrades – I'll never get over working with you – ever. Thank you.

To my adorable pirates: The Captain, The Mate and Ship's Baby (sorry for dropping stuff on you while you slept) – there is no one I'd rather be Ship's Cook for.

To my agent Robert – who took a chance on a writer who almost certainly put the word 'shat' in an email subject line. To my editor Enda who is mercifully immune to swearing for a good cause and in possession of saintly quantities of patience. To Mark Boyle who bravely entered into a correspondence with me. To Bella Bathurst for her time, Amanda Jennings and Marina Hyde for their encouragement and reassurance that I'm not crazy. Professor Mack – for the wisdom and that time you *returned* (from sabbatical).

Remember your bloody manners

I owe a debt of gratitude to the brilliant scientists and journalists who enable people to be informed about what's really happening in our world. I am especially indebted to two news platforms, let's call them the Red One and the Blue One, without their influence, I would not have such a wealth of information to draw on.

Sounds a bit like that echo chamber again, Emma.

Not true – I know they are rigorous and robust sources of information because neither of them will permit me to write for them and they employ lots of brilliant people doing brilliant work. They are the levee against the tidal wave of bullshit that threatens to engulf us all. Thank you.

Thank you also to the scientists. I am so grateful for what you do – thank you for trying to save my kids' lives.

Unlike Putin (he copied reams of his dissertation from other people which I learnt in *How Words Get Good* – Rebecca Lee), I try to acknowledge all of my sources but please forgive me if I have omitted any. I did a lot of research for this project and I average a 14 hour working day with my kids so sometimes I'm a little off my game when I sit down to write at night.

Thank you also to all the writers of books and music. You bring me joy.

E. L. Armstrong is a naturalist who spent her twenties living (and toileting) in the woods, teaching bushcraft and survival skills to men. She has a love of trees, the natural world and upsetting people – but only people who deserve it. Proficient at gutting bunnies, burning trees and digging latrines but guilt-ridden about the above owing to the climate emergency. Despite being handy with an axe, even she knows we can't survive as a species if we keep breaking everything. Emma doesn't *do* social media as she was too busy living outdoors rather than spaffing off about it on Instagram.